LOVING naked

A MEMOIR OF FAITH, HOPE, & COURAGE

MONIQUE BURKS

ISBN 978-1-7378859-4-8 (Softcover Book)
ISBN 978-1-7378859-5-5 (eBook)

Printed in the United States of America

Published by Silversmith Press—Houston, Texas
www.silversmithpress.com

SILVERSMITH
PRESS

Contents

Acknowledgments

I would like to thank first and foremost my Lord and Savior! He has guided me through some dark paths, but at the end of each one there was light. Without Him I am nothing! But because of Him, I have everything I need! He is my rock and salvation!

I would like to give a special thanks to my amazing husband Tracy, my knight in shining armor. You showed me that this broken gracefully aging woman is beautiful. Thank you for loving and supporting me in the moments that were hard for me to even breathe. Thank you to my children: Monique, Nathan, and Joshua. Without you, I could not have learned how strong I really am! You all are gorgeous inside and out, smart and confident. I am thankful that even though you did not choose to go through the journey with me, all three of you gave me all the motivation I needed to keep on going! Thank you, Whitney, my incredible daughter-in-law that always steps in to help me when needed. Thank you for my three adorable grandsons. I learned that this gray-headed "Gami" is important and I still have a purpose. The word love is not enough to say how I feel about my three grandsons. Luke, Nate and Noah, you three have brought me so much joy. I have the greatest blessings with you in my life.

Thank you Mom and Dad (Margo and Alfred) for my good genes and outward personality. Thank you both for loving God and your family. Mom, I am vivacious and determined because of you. Continue to enjoy life because you deserve it. We miss you Dad! Thank you friends, especially my best friends forever Betty and Sylvia and all my friends who supported me through my trials. God knew who I needed and when I needed you. I pray God blesses each one of you for being a blessing to me.

I would like to acknowledge the strong, brave women who wrote excerpts for my book. Thank you for being so transparent, exposed, naked and raw with your true-life story. I know it took courage and I am so honored you shared your story in my book. I know many women will be blessed and healed. Love you bunches!

I would like to thank my church and pastors. You constantly reminded me about my value, that I was full of favor and that my best days are ahead. That what God started in me will be accomplished, my dreams will be completed. Most of all, thank you all for reading my book. May you be blessed!

Credits:
Photography by Victoria Asinovsky of Candy Fox Studio
Hair by Helen in Sugar Land
Nails by Vi at Wanderlust Nail Boutique
Clothing by Margo and Jeanette
Cover design and layout by Chris Boyer

Introduction

Nope. This book is not about naked stuff! It is a PG book. Actually, God wrote this book with the canvas of my lifetime. This book is about real struggles, pain that is indescribable, strength and endurance. We will experience the stripping down to nakedness of pride, confidence, and security. There are raw moments and real exposures of my emotions and experiences that I hope you can relate to. It includes amazing miracles from God! We will laugh, cry, and have some fun! It is jam-packed with favor, mercy, and grace. It was written with love so that you might be inspired during the challenges of your lifetime. I pray it will bring healing in areas that are needed.

I hope this book will guide you through struggles, assist you with decisions, but most of all, help you to make the right choice in a difficult time. Wrong choices are forgiven, but hard to forget. I pray you will have strength and discernment in those difficult moments when it seems so easy to go ahead with selfish desires, or to do wrong knowing what is right. I can promise you God loves us no matter what we do and He has forgiven us and forgets our transgressions, but our human mind cannot forget these things that easily. Some mistakes are never forgotten and can repeat disappointments in us as we replay those memories.

I pray this is not you and that my words offer inspiration to you in those deep moments and in those decisions that are life-impacting.

I have been wanting to write down my thoughts, my valleys, and my successes, but it had to be on God's timing and not mine. I consider myself a well-rounded testimony. I have been through it all! I am not a writer, but God gave me a lot to write about. I kept hearing that "still small voice" inside telling me to write my story. Someone needs to read it. Help someone who is hurting and needs peace! Why hide your valleys under a rock where no one can see them? Let your testimonies be a light for someone's dark moments. Remember that song, This Little Light of Mine, I'm gonna let it shine!? Well, I hope it brings light into your darkness!

It was a journey to understand and fully listen to the "still small voice," the Holy Spirit, but worth every moment. This book is about difficult decisions and unexpected changes. It is about how we go through so much emotionally and that wisdom comes with age. But then the physical challenges come and add to the struggles. I know people say pray (and believe me, that is the number one thing to do). But how do we get from disappointment to resolution while we wait for God's answer? How do we trust and be patient? God tells us to be at peace and rest in Him, but the pain is real.

So how do I walk through it? Wow, the years pass, the challenges do come, and everything does start to transform—especially physically! My body decided it had to change every day. It changed with each struggle and trial I went through. I was not happy with the changes and had to learn to love myself with each change! Each year, each decade, there have been big transformations mentally, physically, and emotionally. I would look at myself and see the effects on my face and my body. It was difficult to accept that I was aging, and life does take a toll on us.

This book is to help those women who experience the changes and valleys in their lives and are disappointed. It is so hard when we go through difficulties, but I can promise you that God has a reason for each one of them. You are only a step away from your victory. I went through love, pain, a difficult pregnancy, divorce, loss, financial struggles, and menopause. Each journey affected me. One constant was knowing God had control, and in his due time, my season would change. My seasons did change, and God showed up each and every time. He gave me double for my trouble and it was amazing every single victory. I pray that the words from my heart and my testimonies will help you appreciate where you are, and who you are, and how you got there, but mostly WHOSE you are! How do we survive? How do we find peace? How do we find joy? How do we breathe when in pain? How does God love us and have us safe in his embrace? How do we wait? Well, here it is. I pray you will be blessed! I pray you learn to love yourself. I pray you get stronger through your storms and use them to bless others. I pray you tune in more to that "still small voice" within us, the Holy Spirit! And I pray you to learn to Love Yourself Naked!

"And we know that all things work together for good to them that love God, to them who are called according to his purpose."

ROMANS 8:28 (KJV)

"Never again will they hunger; never again will they thirst. The sun will not beat down on them, nor any scorching heat. For the Lamb at the center of the throne will be their shepherd; he will lead them to springs of living water. And God will wipe away every tear from their eyes."

REVELATION 7:16-17 (NIV)

"Consider it pure joy, my brothers and sisters, whenever you face trials of many kinds, because you know that the testing of your faith produces perseverance."

JAMES 1:2-3 (NIV)

CHAPTER ONE

Me

I was born in Houston, Texas. We were a large family of seven. My parents had four kids and we were blessed to have Grandma live with us. My parents did it right: girl, boy, girl, boy! I have an older sister and brother, and I had a younger brother who went to heaven at thirty-five. I was the third-born (six years younger than my older brother, and six years older than my younger brother).

As siblings, we were so different. My sister Margo, the oldest, has always been the most reserved. She claims she is the smartest. I still think she is wrong! She is married with two kids and three grandchildren. She is the shortest in our family, while I win the tallest woman in the family trophy (that's not saying much). My older brother Alfred is crazy! He is a character. He makes you laugh constantly and just loves decorating and cars! He is my favorite brother. Oh yeah, I only have one now! He is married with two sons and one grandson! Lots of testosterone in that house. My younger brother, Andre, was a hoot. Now, not too many people might know that word, but it is perfect for him. He was married for twelve years but didn't have any children. He was just happy-go-lucky! He had a big heart and helped others. At his funeral, I remember people crying that we had never met. They all had testimonies on how he helped and assisted them in a time of need. What a legacy!! But he was opinionated. Well, that's a nice way of saying it! We were devastated when the good Lord took him home so early, but we trust in God and in his reasons.

My grandma raised us, and she was amazing! She was a little gray-haired lady who was always humming hymns, and she never complained much about anything. I woke up to the smell of pine cleaner and bacon in the mornings. I would barely be getting out of my bed and she was in there fixing the bed up. I would have to tell her, "Meemo, let me get completely out." She kept us laughing! You could not step out of your clothes without her grabbing them to put in the wash. She was extremely funny, and we loved her. She made delicious fresh homemade tortillas that were amazing. Neighbors would come quickly to eat them when they knew she just made a new batch. They were so good when they were warm and with butter. We loved all her food, especially the fresh brewed iced tea with a full cup of sugar in it! Well, it beat any tea you can buy now. That is why I am so sweet! We were blessed that she lived eighty-three years. She raised my mom on her own. It was not easy in those days for a single mom, but she managed. In those days there were no dishwashers, washing machines, or dryers. People used their two hands to do the work. Thank God I was born in this generation. My mom and grandma were very close. Mom learned so many life lessons from my grandma.

I learned all my cooking skills from Grandma, and to this day I can still remember her in the kitchen. I never did any cooking at home, but I remembered her recipes. Especially at Thanksgiving. That darn turkey would make her so mad because my mom would buy the biggest one out there. It weighed so much for that little lady who cleaned and stuffed it with dressing. She didn't want anyone in her kitchen helping her! It was HER kitchen! Now, she was a godly woman, but had a couple of good names for that turkey! So of course when my mom married, they insisted Grandma would live with them and never work out of the house again! My dad was amazing. He called the place where my grandma worked and said she was not going back. As history has it, Grandma stayed home and never worked again! There was plenty for her to do once we four kids appeared.

My familia has a strong Mexican/French background. It is a great mix! We are all strong-willed. In a room you have to yell to be heard. We are a bit loud. We all think we are right and have many opinions and advice. It does not take much for an argument to start, but once we are done, we just move on to the next subject. We always spend every holiday and birthday together with way too much food. The good thing about so much food is that everybody gets a doggie bag. We can be mad, but we always come together to help each other. Don't tell one family member about your problem because it travels quick! Next thing you know everybody has a solution and advice on how to solve your private problem. Private means nothing in this family. My dad was very European with a strong accent. His accent would make us laugh all the time. He would say things like, "I was 'burn' in San Antonio," and "it's very stranger," and one that we loved was "sounden too muchen." He was very handsome with rosy cheeks. He was so talented; he could sing, dance, play the guitar and loved to tell jokes. He left us to go to heaven a few years ago at the age of ninety. My mom is still at full swing and has always been. At eighty-six, nothing holds her down and she is very passionate. Extremely passionate! She was beautiful and still is. Many people thought she looked like Elizabeth Taylor. She loved dancing and always wears heels even at eighty-six. My parents danced professionally and worked together for thirty-seven years at the Medical Center until they both retired. My dad was her boss—well he thought he was! You don't see that anymore.

As a little girl I was told my father spoiled me. I was his favorite. Just joking! Well not joking, I really was. I had a silk pillow when I was a baby! My parents told me that Dad would invite people from everywhere to come see his princess! I could always go to him for something if Mom said no! To this day I still love my big pool I insisted on. Oh yeah, I got stitches over that one (I fell and hit my head)! My parents decided to buy me a pool for my birthday. Of course, they bought me a kiddie pool that I hated. I insisted on a larger pool for the whole family. While we were on our way to the store to exchange the pool, we had a fender bender and I hit my head. My birthday pictures in my new pool include bandages on my head.

And of course, my boots were great that Mom said I could not have! I wanted white go-go boots so badly, but Mom said no. White go-go boots were really in at that time and I really wanted some. So, I asked Dad and he said yes! Those boots were made for walking! Remember that song? I loved those boots!

We had plenty of ups and downs, but God blessed us and always showed up with grace. Full of passion and drive, I was ready to conquer the world. Blessed to have a walk with God, I was saved at eleven in a big church during summer revival. I'm so happy I was saved because I was going to need God in my life, and I had no idea how much. I was practically born in church. We were always there when the doors opened and even after they had been shut! Church kids! I still love those old hymns in Spanish. I can still smell those wooden pews and that old musty church. I remember those big Easters where we all had to dress up and every family brought food to the church. It seems like every holiday at the church included beans and rice. We were a small church, so I had to be in every play, especially since my mom wrote them. Everything was in Spanish, which at the time I didn't understand, but it all came to me later in life and I appreciate it now.

My parents were married sixty-three years and together for sixty-seven. My mom would get that sparkle in her eyes every time she would look at my dad. So of course,

I assumed my marriage would be like that. I thought my marriage would last that long too! My dad met my mom when she was fourteen and he was twenty-four. He knew instantly he wanted to marry her, especially when he saw her in her baseball outfit. He told us he would see her out and about in different dresses or outfits and every time he asked who that girl was? Grandma knew he wanted to marry her but told him, "You have to wait a few more years; she is only fourteen." Yep, fourteen! They waited three years then they married. She was seventeen and he was twenty-seven. They never had a fight in all those years of marriage. I am fudging a bit. Well, I am fudging a lot. But through thick and thin they stuck it out! Safe to assume my life and marriage would go the same way, right? Especially since my siblings all had successful marriages. My dreams were to be happily in love, one day have children and have joy, joy, joy. Isn't it nice to have an innocent mind in our youth; to believe everything is going to be great, and work out perfectly?

We were your everyday family. Many struggles, laughter, heartaches, fun, fights and oh my God you better keep the house clean! I lived with Mrs. Clean! We were involved in everything at church. I mean everything! We were the family that always helped others. We were the family that held the bridal and baby showers. I watched my parents buy cribs and baby things, and furniture and so much more for those that needed it. My parents would entertain the wealthiest—and those that needed to be fed—all the same way. They showed me to love everyone the same and that

I should also be loved the same. I am so thankful for the lessons we were taught about people. My mom loved the not-so-easy to love. She welcomed all to our home, even some people who were questionable. We were wined and dined by millionaires. My parents worked and retired from Baylor College of Medicine in Houston. Whenever someone ill came in that didn't speak English, they would help them. My parents spoke several languages. We met people from everywhere, mostly affluent because they were here for care at the Medical Center. I never saw my parents act any different with them than they did with so many they fed or helped. It was comforting to have that experience and to be comfortable in anyone's presence and be secure in myself. My parents made sure we had total confidence in who we were and loved others and especially our Lord and Savior! And through our family struggles, my parents showed us that love prevails, you stick it out, you stay strong, committed, and steadfast! They showed us the work ethic we all have today and the determination to accomplish our dreams even if it looked difficult.

We were taught God is still on the throne and never leaves you or forsakes you. All this parenting and learning would be much needed as I made my way into adulthood. I really, really needed it! It would have been great staying young and having a free home, utilities paid, abundance of free groceries, my parents protection, clean clothes always available, and time to just do whatever I wanted with no responsibility. Man, we are in such a hurry to grow up. Why? Life changes so fast and you must grow up. But then you keep growing up! While I was still young and at home, I began to have all these great dreams about my future, my husband, kids, a home, and a great job!

My dreams were starting to take off. I graduated from high school early. The school counselor called me down to the office and said that I had completed all of my credits and that I could stay the next semester if I wanted to, or I could leave. Man, I think I ran out of that school. That allowed me to immediately start tech school for banking. I just knew banking was for me because I always loved the smell of money and counting it since I was very young. I graduated from tech school for banking the night before my high school graduation, which I decided to go back and attend. I had always felt too mature for high school and did not want to attend my graduation, but my mom thought differently so I went. I thought my dreams were forming and things were working out perfectly. My dreams were like a rocket taking off, up and away, but eventually they came down. Came down hard, splashed in the water, then sank and never appeared again. Okay, I might be a drama queen, but I was taught that too! I became a banker and loved it, fell in love, started, going places, loving God! My story begins. I had everything figured out! Yes, awwwwww just perfect!

"You will show me the path of life;
In Your presence is fullness of joy; At Your right hand
are pleasures forevermore."

PSALMS 16:11 (NKJV)

"A man's heart plans his way,
but the Lord directs his steps."

PROVERBS 16:9 (NKJV)

"And I am certain that God, who began the good work
within you, will continue his work until it is finally finished
on the day when Christ Jesus returns."

PHILIPPIANS 1:6 (NLT)

"Glory in his holy name; let the hearts of those who
seek the Lord rejoice. Look to the Lord and his strength;
seek his face always."

PSALMS 105:3-4 (NIV)

CHAPTER TWO

Thought He Was The Right Man

Sometimes it might look good or feel right, but it is not! We do learn some of this relationship stuff much easier as we age, but unfortunately for most of us, we fall in love and marry young and dumb. We definitely use our emotions instead of wisdom and knowledge, and lust is a huge factor in our relationships. We mistake lust for love. If only I had the wisdom and knowledge then, that I have now. The discernment that I learned eventually would have made a difference. But God knew what He was doing and why and when He was doing it. As a Christian serving in church, I thought I was prepared to meet my mate and live happily ever after!

So, I fall madly in love, finally. Ready, set, go! I married at twenty-one. Things seemed right and we were prepared. Prepared is such a mature word! We really are never quite prepared for the changes and struggles we will endure. I knew my husband to be when we were young from church. We had lost touch when my family moved churches, but one day, we saw each other at a ball game and things changed. He basically had the same background as me. His parents were married forever. They are still married to this day, and it has been sixty-plus years. Wow. Still married to this day! Now please don't think this is an easy task. It takes a lot of love and tenacity. We were serving at the church where we both attended. His dad was my Sunday school teacher and his mom the church secretary. My dad was the choir director and my mom a teacher. Just perfect! He had two older brothers, both also engaged and heading to the altar and the wonderful married life. Yes, three brothers, three fiancées. His parents were serving the Lord, my parents were serving the Lord. I am a Christian, he is a Christian. Hey, it's going to be perfect. Right? We knew each other at church since we were very young. Our families knew each other forever so it had to be perfect!

We dated for a year before we were married. We had a great relationship. We saw each other almost every day. He constantly bought me things. He was kind and attentive which is exactly what I expected from a nice, young, Christian man. He worked hard and had great plans for his future. He was sent out of the state to work, and we really missed each other. You know the saying: "Distance makes the heart grow fonder." He would send money so I could start preparing for our future (well, mostly for my ring). Oh, the ring is so important! We were both ready. We prepared for the big wedding day, excited to be in love, and it was oh so much fun! Church, pastor, flowers, dresses, invitations, food, music... well mariachis in this case. We put so much emphasis on the wedding and not on the marriage. If we could have slowed down and worked on the marriage part more before we married, it could have saved us from some mistakes. I wore my mom's beautiful wedding dress that was close to thirty years old. Oh, it is still beautiful to this day! It was made with imported Italian silk. The train was so long that two little girls had to carry it. The beading on it was gorgeous. It weighed a ton. My daddy really spoiled my mom with such a beautiful wedding dress. I thought for sure after wearing her dress and looking like a princess I would be married at least sixty-four years too! The music started in the church, the doors opened, and I saw him. I felt sick. No... not nervous... sick. At that moment, I felt like he was not the one. Something internal was speaking to me but I wasn't obeying. My dad, who was so proud of me, had been a little apprehensive of my marriage, but eventually he came around. On that beautiful day he walked me down that long aisle. It felt like an eternity! It was a long walk to the altar. Immediately, I felt something come over me and I told Daddy that I couldn't do this. I had not learned to pay attention to that "still small voice" inside of me yet! I wished I had! I would have been the runaway bride! Of course, my dad explained how most brides and grooms get nervous and it would be okay. By then, we reached the altar. So, I married him!

You see, we had an argument the day before and basically did not speak during rehearsal or dinner. Money is one of the biggest stressors in marriage, and that's exactly what we fought over. Hey, it's not easy combining accounts! I had to change my name. What! I eventually felt better about it. Well, somewhat. Men get so funky about you having to change your name and all the submissive stuff kicks in fast and we were not even married yet! Then, having to combine accounts was not easy especially when I brought more to the account. I got a good glimpse of some quick changes happening, and they did worry me a bit. (This is where marriage counseling can help!) The wedding went on. We married, ate, danced, and had fun! After we married, we went on a romantic honeymoon. NOT! I enjoyed watching him snorkel, parasail, scuba dive, and anything else he enjoyed. I was the not-so-happy newlywed on the beach. I felt like a whale just sitting and waiting; lonely on a beach in a beautiful tropical paradise. He had a great time! Romance? Nope. Sex? Barely. And love all out the window. I thought we would spend more time in the room. I was hoping! My dreams had this part planned differently. When we returned home, we settled into life. Well, not exactly what I expected either. Off the bat there were strange things happening.

As women, we have intuition that can drive us crazy! Early on, he was coming home late and making excuses about his car or job. Once, he smelled like beer and said he had one while he was fixing his car! I remember sitting there in my living room and dinner was ready. I was all pretty and smelling good and he came home late again. No romance, no kiss. He did not even acknowledge me. It was so hurtful. I can remember another time when he made a huge decision on changing jobs that we never even talked about together. My radar went up quickly, and I began to see that I did not know much about this man I had married.

As time went on, we enjoyed traveling, we ate out as much as we wanted, bought our first new home within months, then sold it and built a second new home. We had two cars, two dogs, and the pretty two-story house in the cul-de-sac with the nice trimmed green grass. We did not worry much about money because we both had good jobs. We enjoyed great holidays and loved spending time with our families, we went to church, and things were normal. Everything seemed perfectly normal. But did I mention my husband thought the grass was greener on the other side? Yes. Even with all the great stuff, it was not enough for him. I found out my husband had someone else only a year into our marriage.

Devastation kicked in. My gut was right! I had already seen some differences and felt like he was not all that into me. Even on the honeymoon I could feel that things had changed. Okay, this is a crazy story I was not going to write, but it is just so perfect. While on our honeymoon in Ixtapa, we went from one island to another on a small boat. I was sitting there smiling, thinking hey, I'm a newlywed in love! This female native of the island was sitting at the end of the boat. She was a very large woman and very intimidating and I was sitting right across from her. She just kept staring at me. I felt a little uncomfortable, but I could not move anywhere! Finally, she spoke and asked me if we were on our honeymoon. (In Spanish of course! Yes, I'm bilingual.) Proudly, I said yes! Nothing could have prepared me for her response. She leaned over close to my face and told me, "As soon as you get home, slap his face as hard as you can!"

Of course, I was shocked and said, "Why? He has not done anything to warrant that." She responded with, "Slap him for all the things he is going to do to you!" WOW! Maybe that was the "still small voice" again.

We returned home and it turned out that she was absolutely right about him. Instantly, life changed and the pain and hurt began. Self-confidence, self-respect, and self-love started to get stripped away from me. Radar up! Radar right! It was an interesting way of finding out about his first affair. Remember those little pink sticky Post-It notes? Well, one got stuck in my toilet and it was from his girlfriend. I sat down to pee and there it was stuck in the hole of the toilet bowl. I'm so glad I saw it before I peed. Of course, as a woman I was curious, so I pulled it out and to my surprise, signed "with love" was a note expressing excitement to see him later that night. Shocked and so hurt, I just wanted to scream and cry. Later I found out that other people already knew and had seen pictures of them together. Why did they not tell me? We live in such a small world and it ended up that he was dating a friend of my sister-in-law's cousin. Did you follow that one? Well, that cousin worked for me and just could not bear to tell me. We rode to work together every day and she knew I was skeptical and felt something was wrong. She knew all the time. She literally saw a picture of them together. Why not tell that person if you see it happening? It saves so much time, pain, and humiliation. *What did I do? Do I stay? Does he leave? What? What? What? And why did people not tell me?* Unfaithfulness is ugly. It destroys, it cuts down. It is abusive. Maybe not physically, but it affects you in the same way. It occupies all your time just trying to figure out why!

You see, I was only twenty-two and I was already starting to scar on the inside and see myself as not attractive on the outside. I started thinking back, what could I have done differently to make him happy? Did I need to lose weight? Maybe dye my hair? Did I need to do something, anything to change what happened? Where did I lack? Maybe my cooking, my family, something... but what? I had no idea how difficult it would get or what damage it would cause me. How I would become exposed with raw emotions that I could not understand. How I would become stripped naked of everything! Every bit of confidence, pride and security would soon be ripped out of my life. I was a newlywed and should have been enjoying my husband, my life, and my youth. Unfortunately, he robbed me of my youth. Those years were stolen from me. I was young and physically I still looked good. I was lean and firm, not gray. I still had the energy to run, have fun and enjoy sex. Instead, my days were spent full of anxiety, fear, worry, and lack. I turned against myself; saw myself as unattractive, fat, and ugly. Later I would realize it is the devil who comes to kill, steal, and destroy, but I blamed my husband mostly at that point. My self-image was slowly being diminished. The devil was slowly killing all of my joy, stealing all of my days, and destroying all that I was. So, I began the next part of my journey looking for different answers. How can I fall in love with me again? How can I follow the "still small voice?" How could I be accepted for who I was?

*"The Lord saves the righteous and protects them
in times of trouble."*

PSALMS 37:39 (GNT)

"Cast all your anxiety on him because he cares for you."

1 PETER 5:7 (NIV)

*"But those who trust in the Lord will find new strength.
They will soar high on wings like eagles. They will run and
not grow weary. They will walk and not faint."*

ISAIAH 40:31 (NLT)

CHAPTER THREE

Secret Betrayal

We decided to seek counseling like most couples. We went to Christian counseling. We went to professional counseling. We spoke to pastors and mentors. Friends spoke to us, to him, to me. I prayed and hoped. We decided to try and work on it. He, of course, made promises to be a faithful husband. We continued living each day, celebrating holidays and birthdays, and we kept moving forward in our marriage. I thought we were trying to make it work. But it was hard for me to forgive, harder to forget, and even harder to be intimate with him. Every time I had to undress in front of him, I hated it. I am sure many women know that feeling, making sure the lights are off, dressing in the closet. I felt so unattractive. I did not feel sexy at all. Intimacy had already been a problem for us, but it became much more difficult. The devil has a way of deceiving you; I literally saw myself as fat in a 100-pound body. In my mind, every time he touched me or I was laying there with him, I was thinking, *I'm not enough. Was he thinking of her? Were there more women? What was it about her that I didn't have? How do I move on? How do I ever make love to this man again and enjoy it?*

As time passed, we managed to work it out...or rather I worked things out. Things seemed better, with a few suspicions, but I lived in denial. It was easier that way. We seemed to be a happy couple just enjoying ourselves. After about five years he wanted children, and I soon began to feel the same. Early on, I had not been sure about having a family, but when I was finally ready, I wanted it to happen fast! I thought *Hey, he is into me again so why not start a family?* We had been married for five years, so it seemed like the right time. We were financially stable; we had a home and we seemed happy. Love really is blind though and sometimes we just don't want to see some things and prefer to stay in denial. My gut kept bugging me because there were still some weird things happening with him. Those same little signs and situations like before, but I tried to move on. My husband always had excuses for coming home late. He wasn't very loving and attentive. His character changed and this led to loveless sex. Though we were trying to have a baby, I don't think it was out of love on his part. We tried to get pregnant to no avail. It took about a year of fertility shots, minor procedures and a lot of prayer.

Finally, we were pregnant. My excitement almost cleared all of the awful memories away. It was amazing being told you're having a baby. Nothing else seemed to matter. Soon though, the pregnancy turned tough, real tough. Man, all I did was vomit. The first trimester I was the skinniest pregnant woman around. There was nothing I could keep down.

I spent a good bit of time going to the doctor or emergency room for visits. This baby was going to make it tough on me, but I was prepared and ready. My husband was a good provider financially, I can't lie, but he was gone a lot. My radar unfortunately kept going off. There were still times he was late coming home, sometimes smelling of beer. I would call the police station where he worked, but he would not be there and had not shown up for his shift. He would tell me he had worked late. Then, seven months into the pregnancy, the baby, who we did not know at the time was a girl, tried to come early. I was sitting at work and I began having labor pains. I called my doctor and he told me to go to the hospital quickly. Wow! Injections of all kinds were quickly pumped into me as soon as I arrived at the hospital. One medicine they injected me with was to stop the labor and I felt like someone had kicked me hard in the face. This feeling was only a part of the side effects but it did not feel very good. I was placed on complete bedrest and all I could do was wait on my little angel to be born as I laid there getting fatter.

May 9th finally arrived, little Miss Wonderful was born, and we were both so excited. She was beautiful! Labor was a nightmare. I went to the hospital the day before feeling so sick. By early morning, I was in full labor and eighteen hours later she was born. I forgot about all the pain, injections, and all those unknown people that kept poking and checking me. All the pain and hemorrhaging was worth it. My husband seemed to be very happy and loved his little girl. However, things changed after only a few months. My husband was at home physically but not emotionally. He was not interested in me or attentive to our marriage. It can be so difficult to put into words the female intuition that kicks in. It's not always the best thing, but it is usually right. And I had felt this before. I began to feel the difference in our relationship and felt that there was someone else consuming his time. Eventually, I found out in the middle of my pregnancy that he left me to go to a topless joint. Here I was pregnant, feeling fat and flabby, and on top of that, what an insult to find out your husband had to go see naked women instead of supporting the pregnant one he has at home. This happened time and time again. One day when he dumped me at the in-laws to visit and he left me there for hours. I sat there just waiting for him to come back and pick me up. I had no idea where he was. Later, I found a reciept. He had spent the day at a local topless joint not far from his parent's house. One time he even forgot me at the dentist. While I was pregnant, I needed to have a procedure on my teeth. He drove me there and dropped me off. When I was finished at the dentist, I sat there for hours waiting on him. He showed up smelling like beer and I was not very happy. How could he just go have fun and not care about picking me up on time. What was going on? Who was taking his time? Why? I did not understand. Again, I felt so broken and hurt. Every time he left, I thought for sure he was going to another topless joint or to go see someone. Unless you've been there, it's hard to understand what goes through your mind and the pain that comes with the experiences. My first thought was, *My body was not good enough.*

I didn't think he loved me because *how could he leave me for hours like that! How could he show up smelling like beer and be completely happy while I sat there hurt and miserable? Where is the love and respect? Doesn't the sacrifice of nine months, all the vomiting, pain, shots, hospital emergency visits mean anything? Did my body change that much from pregnancy that I was repulsive or what?* You see, his job was a police officer so I never knew if he was working or not. I would just assume it was work, but I had no idea.

I was a new mom, busy and totally content with my baby girl. Not even trying to keep up with his hours or his whereabouts. The occasional smell of beer on him or reports from others that they "saw him with someone" continued. I tried to tune it all out so I could focus on my bundle of joy. I loved our baby girl. When I went back to work at the bank, I was only there about two hours and I missed her terribly. She was my world so I decided to quit my job to stay home with her. I walked right over and told my supervisor I couldn't leave my baby girl. It is crazy how you can love so deeply! There was no way I could not be with my angel every moment. Best decision ever! I made a lot of sacrifices since I wasn't working, like no car for two years, but it was worth it. I was so happy, just being a mom.

"He" was a good dad. He was attentive to our little girl, just not to me. Since he was trying to work extra to make up for my lost income, we did not have much time together. He claimed he was working more hours and taking jobs but I could never be certain. Soon after I found out that my husband was again interested in someone else. Wow, really? You think that the second time it wouldn't hurt as much. Nope. It still hurt very much! I was constantly sick to my stomach about my husband. I started blaming myself, thinking it must be my fault and that maybe I was not that attractive anymore. It was a terrible place to be. I just wanted to love and cuddle my baby, but I was broken into so many pieces. I just played in my mind over and over the things that happened wondering, did I do something wrong? What could I do? Could I do anything to fix it? Every negative emotion kicked in: fear, anxiety, shame. All I could do was pray to God to please help! More hurt, more scars! I hated myself and seeing my body naked.

"Humble yourselves, therefore, under God's mighty hand, that he may lift you up in due time. Cast all your anxiety on him because he cares for you."

1 PETER 5:6-7 (NIV)

"We can rejoice, too, when we run into problems and trials, for we know that they help us develop endurance. And endurance develops strength of character, and character strengthens our confident hope of salvation. And this hope will not lead to disappointment. For we know how dearly God loves us, because he has given us the Holy Spirit to fill our hearts with his love."

ROMANS 5:3-5 (NLT)

CHAPTER FOUR

Growing Family, Growing Apart

Time passed and things seemed better. He convinced me nothing was happening. Now this sounds like a cliché, but when you are married with a baby, you try hard to believe it's all working out. We seemed to be doing better, and I believed him when he said he was trying! We discussed having another child about a year after Monique was born. Of course, I felt a bit cautious because I went through so much the first time during my pregnancy and labor. Plus, it wasn't easy to forget the hurt from our past problems which made me wonder if I should have another child with him. But soon after, I was pregnant again. This time I had no problem getting pregnant. We decided to find out the gender and to our surprise, it was a boy! Twenty-two months after our little girl, we had a gorgeous little boy that we named Nathan. I had a perfect pregnancy; the only problem was he came two weeks late. I had a super short labor and finally my son arrived. Oh, I remember the joy of his little face and holding both my angels. God had blessed me so much, how could anything go wrong?

As life would have it, things did go wrong. One day a few months later, I had a party with friends and family. I had some home videos on a big black VHS tape I wanted to share with everyone and gathered them around the television. I had my brother-in-law put the video in the machine and hit play... and oh my! It wasn't a family video like I thought—it was a porn movie. Yes, this happened in front of a room full of family and friends. I was totally embarrassed and felt betrayed all over again. It wasn't the first time I found porn in the house. I remember once I found a magazine taped behind the toilet tank. Luckily, I am very thorough in my cleaning!

I know some people might be fine with porn or girlie magazines, but I am not. I especially don't like when it's something kept hidden from me. Porn is a bad seed of destruction, and when planted, it will grow. Marriage is about two people and two people only. Porn is a lie. Sexual energy expressed outside of the marriage in unfaithfulness. It is a way for the devil to enter and destroy marriages. Men should respect their wives and vice versa. Women who feel that this behavior has no place in their relationship need to set boundaries early on. Marriage is a commitment between two people, for better or worse. Porn is particularly degrading to women and it had already caused so much trouble in our marriage. Why was this happening again? Why couldn't he be content and committed to me? Why had this happened in a room full of people? I felt so embarrassed, so humiliated, so exposed! I felt naked in a room full of family and friends. I remember taking my kids and going home with my sister-in-law and brother-in-law. I just needed space and time to think. I couldn't help but think *here we go again. This is my second pregnancy so it must be my body changes that he doesn't like! He can't stand looking at me, so he resorts to porn.* It was so easy to blame myself. The devil loves deceiving us. After this incident, things never improved much. I knew in my heart that I wanted a man to respect me completely. I deserved that! It was so hard to continue being with him, but unfortunately, he was still my husband. I knew that biblically I needed to make this work and intimacy was a part of marriage. However, by this point we were hit-and-miss sexually, I did not trust him, and I was just too busy with my two angels.

As the Lord would have it, one of our rare intimate encounters lead to the birth of another cute little boy named Joshua nineteen months later. I had another perfect pregnancy and labor. I was so complete. My three angels were the cutest babies ever (I'm not bias). Joshua was born right before Christmas, and it was the best gift I could have asked for. I didn't care about my current circumstances, I was just so blessed. Oh, how I loved them! It was mesmerizing being a mom. Even after they would break things, color on furniture, argue, and run all over the house, I was devoted and would protect them and be there for all their needs forever. I would die for them!

We seemed to enjoy our kids but not necessarily with the two of us together at the same time. Sometimes he would stay out all night. My friends would go check on his car at the police station, but it wasn't there. Of course, he would still tell me he had been at work all night. There was no longer any intimacy between us. Things quickly escalated, our separation grew greater, and so did my concerns. It started when he got me a pager. Do you remember those gadgets? I thought it was sweet that he wanted to keep up with me. He would beep me constantly and I would call him to tell him where I was. Turns out, he just wanted to make sure that we wouldn't run into each other while he was out with another woman. So many things were happening all at once and I couldn't help but just cry quietly to myself. He had been seen in public with women, no longer cared about coming home, and he wasn't even trying to be kind or respectful at that point. I did not want my babies to feel my pain, so I kept my chin up... what else could I do? I was pretty sure my whole marriage was headed south. I began thinking of the potential financial stress of having only one income with three children, so I even worked a little to help with the children's needs. Avon, Mary Kay, Jafra, oh yes Tupperware! I could no longer just be a housewife without contributing financially. I had some eventful moments working while having three little ones, but I always kept on going. One of my jobs was selling Tupperware. When I had to go downtown to pick up my orders, my three children went with me. It was quite difficult putting three kids in a small car and stuffing it with all my Tupperware orders, but it worked, and I got the job done. Then I decided to sell Mary Kay and Jafra, both of which are makeup companies. The makeup was so much easier to haul around. My third job was selling Avon; they had little catalogs that you would hang on front door handles of a home. I remember one day I was hanging a catalog at one of my neighbors' homes and a Doberman Pincher came after me. I had no idea I could run that fast! Boy, did I run and scream! Thank God my babies were all in the car. Those jobs didn't make me very much money, but I enjoyed the experience.

One time, I had a credit card I designated for the children's Christmas gifts. I was so excited and prepared to enjoy shopping without stressing over money. I went to the store to buy the gifts with the three kids in tow. We had a nice day but when I got to the register, my card was declined. I was standing there with my three kids feeling totally embarrassed. My cart was full of gifts I picked out. Imagine, dressing three kids, taking them all to the store, trying to look for gifts, and hauling the gifts to the register and then not being able to pay for them. I asked if they could run the card a second time. How could this be? I told the cashier there must have been a mistake because I knew there was a zero balance. Well, she ran the card a second time and it was declined again. Wow, I felt awful. We did not have cell phones yet, so I had to wait to get home and call my credit card company from my home phone. Sure enough, there were charges I didn't know about that maxed out the card, and one charge for over $300 at a topless joint! I was devastated! There are no words to describe how mad I was. How depressing. How wrong! Yes. I found a way to get those presents. As I said earlier, my three children were not going to suffer. I was going to make sure that they were happy! Thank God for my parents as they helped me buy my children's Christmas gifts.

I would talk to my best friends and neighbors about what was happening, and they were like "no way!" I needed support, I was slowly losing myself as a woman, as a human! I prayed and cried and prayed. But these were those rough times where we must wait on God! It is a very hard position to be in. We want answers and we want them now! This is the time for a trust that comes with God's promise, to put it at his feet at his throne of grace, and let go, let God, until the answer comes. It's not easy but we have to keep on breathing, keep on marching, keep on surviving until we see that glimmer of hope we are waiting for. Everyone I shared with said we looked like the perfect happy suburban family. Yes, we looked that way. It was hard to get support because people just could not believe it. I was amazed at the perception that people had of my situation even though I was broken inside.

I decided to speak to my parents' pastor and his wife. They both agreed I had to try and make the marriage work. Both said divorce was wrong and I had to think about the kids. They said to put myself out there more sexually and be more attentive to him. So, despite what I felt, I kept trying my best to be a great mom and to be a sexy wife, but nothing really seemed to matter. It was so degrading. I kept my home clean, cooked, washed clothes, loved working on my yard and gardening but he still was not interested. I had done everything I knew to do so I believed the problem was me. I wasn't attractive anymore. My body was different. I had my three pregnancies, and I reached the end of my romance years. My pretty years were gone. There were no more cute, short dresses, no more fun. No more bikinis, only a sad disappointing one-piece. Why would he look at me? I looked like a tired mom! There was nothing worse than sitting at the pool seeing young women in bikinis walk by with their "perfect" bodies. In my mind I was still blaming myself, my body, my changes. I was disappointed and sad. I had to keep on going strong because my family needed me, so there was no self-pity time. The lies, excuses and coming home late continued. There were more scars, more hurt, lies, disrespect, more of me thinking it was me. I didn't look like the girls in the magazines, I couldn't compete with them! I was all done!

I was a little thing weighing in around 108 pounds, not much bigger than when we married. Still, I saw myself as being fat, and my husband would tell me I was fat. But the devil is a liar. The devil had me believing all kinds of negativity about myself and my body. He would whisper in my ear and I would believe everything he said. Things continued to get ugly. Lack of respect, insults, threats that he was moving out. More suspicions. More lies. More late nights. Sometimes he didn't come home until early morning. Wow, long hours at work huh? Sure, I was a homebody with a new physical body after having three children. Maybe I was boring and uneventful. Could I blame him? I didn't even know the woman I saw in the mirror any longer. Things on my body shifted, expanded, and dropped. It is hard on women when we start seeing changes and the body is not working with you anymore. It is even harder when your husband is busy looking at everything else but you. It was harder and harder to love myself naked or just love myself... period!

When the righteous cry for help, the Lord hears and delivers them out of all their troubles. The Lord is near to the brokenhearted and saves the crushed in spirit.

PSALMS 34:17-18 (ESV)

The LORD is my light and salvation; whom shall I fear? The LORD is the strength of my life; of whom shall I be afraid?

PSALMS 27:1 (KJV)

For I am the Lord your God who takes hold of your right hand and says to you, Do not fear, I will help you.

ISAIAH 41:13 (NIV)

The Beginning Of The End

My days were spent cleaning, cooking, washing, grocery shopping, playtime, playgrounds, watching every kid movie we could own. This was quite different from my past. As I mentioned earlier, I was in banking before I was married. I enjoyed being a branch manager/assistant vice president. I always moved quickly to the top at all my jobs. I really enjoyed that and the money! I was respected and listened to. I made decisions and people accepted them. I fired and hired. I went to socials and meetings. I traveled and had status. My name plate was on my big desk in my big office! I loved dressing up and makeup, shoes and more shoes. Bling and more bling!

After having children, my attire changed as much as my body did. I would wear the first thing I could find which was mostly something that my kids could yank on, spit up on, or get dirty. My new social outings were at the local fast-food joints! Chicken nuggets and fries please! I no longer had my business status, I was just mom. But I was totally happy and content with that; I loved those three little angels and did not really miss anything about working. Well, maybe the cute little dresses! I learned the art of cooking and crafting. We did all kinds of stuff; we painted, we ran outside and just laughed. Yes, as a full-time mom. I was happy spending every moment with my children. I stress this because things changed again, and these moments would become so importantly impressed in my memory. I felt like this was what I was born to do! I loved being a mom! Dad, on the other hand, would continue to get home later and later and later. I felt the coldness and distance between us and so much animosity.

Again, I looked at myself and thought maybe I was to blame. I was so busy being a mom, not a wife. I definitely was not romantic or sexy – that had faded away. I was tired. Actually, better said, I was exhausted. I talked mom, I walked mom, I definitely dressed mom. I was a mom! You see, you can do all the right things, but it is not good enough. We had a clean home, I made homecooked meals, we had three adorable kids, and still, it was not enough for him.

Then one day my daughter told me something I wasn't prepared to hear. She told me that Daddy brought a friend to lunch at school to see her. What!! Not only was I feeling diminished as a woman, but now my space was being invaded and it was affecting my children. Of course, when I asked him about it later that night, he said it was a teacher. Sure! It was getting tough for him to lay low, prancing around with the new one.

Around that time, his job called to tell me he had a minor injury at work and had to be taken to the hospital. Of course, I panicked! I called the hospital only to be told his wife was already there with him! Really! Explain that one on the phone! When I told the nurse that I was his wife, she was totally embarrassed for me. Needless to say, I didn't bother going to the hospital. When he came home that night, it did not go very well. I was totally embarrassed for myself and those raw emotions just cut through me. I was so humiliated, so exposed. I asked him about it, but he really did not care how I felt. Having your feelings dismissed is so painful. I can't explain the knife that I felt cut through my heart, my mind, my everything. At that moment I was just battered. You see abuse is abuse. Physical, mental or emotional it still hurts the same! Again, my gut started hurting and deeper scars formed, the pain got worse, and the feeling that I was just not good enough became overwhelming. My children were one, three, and five years old and needed a lot of my time and attention. I needed time for myself—prayer time, quiet time, but it was not going to happen.

By this time in the marriage, I stayed upstairs sleeping with my children, and we were inseparable. He was hardly ever home anymore, so we did not miss sleeping together. Things started going downhill from there, really fast. I was trying to gear up my kids to love God, praying things would change. But nothing changed. The constant late nights and patronizing continued. There is nothing worse than constantly being told by your husband that you are not loved anymore and that you are not attractive. I just wanted to be happy and give my kids a great future. It was not going to happen the way I planned. I wanted them to have Mommy and Daddy together at the same home. There was so much going through my mind.

I prayed. Oh, how I prayed. My friends at church and family laid hands on me and prayed. I knew I had to make this work somehow. I just wanted my joy restored and my self-respect. I spoke to so many people and received mentoring from pastors. I searched tirelessly for help. I needed God to fix this now! Don't we just want it done fast and our way? God had his purpose for every situation, and we must wait, learn, and pray! Help me love myself Lord! Just help me, Lord!

As I prayed, and hoped for a good outcome, it continued to get worse. I knew it did not look promising. I was in waiting mode and I did not like that position. But I had no other choice. God does not give us more than we can handle, though we might indeed think it is too much. God gives us the strength to get by moment by moment. He is in control! He keeps his tender arms around us at all times.

As I loved and enjoyed my children, my husband was busy enjoying other women. It seemed constant by this time. People knew, people saw him, people were feeling sorry for me. It is horrible and humiliating to be pitied. We grew apart and intimacy was a thing of the past, even though the past was not all that great either. There were rumors and suspicions, and it started to go from bad to worse. He had been threatening to leave for a long time but now his threats were almost daily—yet he still kept showing up! Day after day, he kept coming home telling me, "I am leaving you." He would say, "Today is the day. I am about to leave!" What a head-trip! And so painful! I just was paralyzed in fear daily. My self-image was at the lowest possible. Anxiety kicked in and I lost weight, I lost dignity and felt just plain ugly. The hurt and fear of what to do overwhelmed me. He would tell me I was not attractive, that I was fat. It was a constant knock-down from him. He would tell me that he would leave me alone with nothing, and then he would take the kids. That was my biggest fear – not my kids, please Lord. Each day he would tell me the divorce papers were on their way and I was going to be served. I would spend days looking out the window or checking behind me waiting to see if papers would be served, while trying to laugh and play with my babies. Imagine me thinking what good would I be to my kids with no job, no money, no husband, no father at home, broken inside and completely inadequate as a woman. It was awful to be raising three children and watching and waiting for the worst to happen. I cried in seclusion. There was no way I could let my babies see me hurt. Slowly, but surely, I dwindled as a woman and as a human. I could not understand why someone would deliberately hurt me. I felt so alone even though at this point my closest friends and family were starting to see what was happening and giving me love and support.

I knew God was still in control and that He had a great plan for me and my sweet angels, but I was hurting so bad.

It was so unfair. Why did my babies have to endure pain, why me? I waited and waited and waited, but no divorce papers would come. I waited on answers to my prayers, but nothing came. He kept threatening me that he was leaving. It happened every day! It was awful. I know God does not give us more than we can bear, but I was thinking that was just too much!

As the days went on he continued with more insults, bringing me more pain, more scars, and more of me not being able to love myself! But still the papers never came. He would not leave. I kept wondering, What is happening? Oh, it has to be me! Even in my brokenness, I spent a lot of time praying that somehow it would all go away—that he would somehow love me again, and walk through the door asking for forgiveness. I prayed through my tears for my happily ever after. I would dream that he would see me as beautiful! I had adopted a daily prayer, I would hold my hands out and say, "Lord empty my hands of what I don't need," then lift them to heaven and say, "Fill my hands with what I do need" I didn't know at the time, but God was listening and He had a better plan for my life than anything I could have designed on my own.

...Don't be dejected and sad, for the joy of the Lord is your strength!

NEHEMIAH 8:10 (NLT)

I will go before you and make the crooked places straight

ISAIAH 45:2 (NKJV)

Do not be anxious about anything, but in every situation, by prayer and petition with thanksgiving, present your requests to God. And the peace of God, which transcends all understanding, will guard your hearts and your minds in Christ Jesus.

PHILIPPIANS 4:6-7 (NIV)

Blessed is the one who perseveres under trial because, having stood the test, that person will receive the crown of life that the Lord has promised to those who love him.

JAMES 1:12 (NIV)

CHAPTER SIX

Taking Out The Trash

Five months passed and he was still warning about serving me divorce papers, but none had arrived. He would not leave. The house was totally uncomfortable. I was sick thinking he might not ever come back and sick thinking he would be back soon. Imagine living that way daily. I began to think I would be better off without him. He even suggested that we could share the house; I could live upstairs with my children, and he could live downstairs. He said we could date and have separate lives. Wow, what a dear! Not! Things came to a head two days before Thanksgiving when he had not come home again. I was feeling badly for the kids, so I called him and said, "Hey you got kids, they need you." He told me that we really were not together anymore, so he did not have to come home. I told him, "You still have kids."

I knew it was time for a change when my daughter asked me one day, "Mommy, why don't I see Mommy and Daddy together?" That cut me to the core. It was right around Thanksgiving. I had taken the kids to my mother's house for dinner. He was invited but I didn't know if he would show up or not. But right as we sat down to say the blessing, he did. He walked in the door, sat down at the table next to me, grabbed my hands and joined in that family prayer. Now, I was and am a Christian woman, but really. Was he serious? Did he think he would just walk in and act like nothing ever happened? Did he have his mistress waiting in the car? That's right he should pray—He'd better call on Jesus now!

That was the final blow. I was hurt, I was sad, I was MAD! Coincidentally I had just spoken to a pastor who advised me to "throw out the trash from my home." This might sound harsh, and non-Christian, but he saw the damage that was occurring to me and my children. Others told me to "Hang in there," or "Try to look sexy," or "Bake for him." Try, try, try, they told me! As if that would do anything. He was hardly home to know if I was looking sexy, or baking or what!. Plus, I was exhausted raising three small children and had very busy days. I did not feel sexy at all and was too hurt to want to bake anything. So, the following Sunday after Thanksgiving when he again did not come home until the early morning, I made my move. Better put... God moved me!

What happened next could only have been arranged by God. He stepped in right before I thought I would go crazy! My victory was in front of me, but I had to be still and wait. This was my ordained destiny, not everyone's. I knew God was moving me toward something. I had to take action. I had to stand up for myself—to protect my kids and get free from the pain and abuse. So...I did it, I kicked him out! Now, for many, that might sound harsh, but it took a lot of guts. One night, I had gotten up at 2:00 a.m. and he was not home, so I had my wonderful neighbors write a letter to him on their computer saying it was time for him to exit. They printed it and I went into action. I packed his clothes neatly in suitcases and placed them outside with the letter and locked up the house and went to sleep. (My friends were more upset because I packed his clothes neatly in our Samsonite luggage instead of trash bags. Never thought I would have to do this. A few hours later he came home and came upstairs and said to me, "Is this what you want?" I said, "This is what you want." He locked the door and left, that was it. The letter I wrote said this: *I am tired, and I do not want to live this way. If you want to be a husband and father stay, if not go. I can't do this anymore you never coming home, my kids seeing me sad, mad, broken and the women. So done, no more!*

I had been feeling miserable about myself and he had minimized me to nothing and then this happened. Of course, all my family and friends were shocked. I was at home with no job and three young kids. But I knew I needed a change. A big one! Everyone wondered how I would survive. I wondered how I would survive. I was a mother of three with no job, no husband, no self-respect, no nothing! I was just not loving myself at all. I was totally broken. Everyone knew. I was exposed to all. I was standing there naked, stripped of everything, the pain was so intense, so raw! But I was so glad God always loved me. I was so blessed that He had me in the palm of his hands. I was so grateful for a God of mercy, for my crown of favor, for grace, wonderful grace.

All I could think about were my kids. How was I going to raise them alone? How would I provide for them? How would I mend this broken life? How would I love myself, this lifeless being; this aging woman who had nothing? How would I erase the constant negative recordings in my head? But God! He can remove all stains! He repairs! He gives us double for our trouble! He never leaves us or forsakes us!

Return to the stronghold, you prisoners of hope. Even today I declare that I will restore double to you.

ZECHARIAH 9:12 (NIV)

Because you got a double dose of trouble and more than your share of contempt, Your inheritance in the land will be doubled and your joy go on forever.

ISAIAH 61:7 (MSG)

"For I know the plans I have for you," declares the Lord, "plans to prosper you and not to harm you, plans to give you hope and a future."

JEREMIAH 29:11 (NIV)

Facing Reality

It did not take long for reality to set in. It probably took about four hours. He showed up in his girlfriend's SUV to pick up some of his stuff. It was like a slap in the face. Let's bring her vehicle, why not! He took some clothes and acted like nothing was wrong. Then he wanted to spend time with the kids. He went upstairs and watched TV with them like it was nothing. I thought *what now? I have to share my precious angels with this monster?* I was totally frustrated and mad! He humiliated me by all his actions and then left. It was quite eerie! I just knew it was over completely. The next morning, I found out I was broke. He had the nerve to go to the bank and close all accounts. Yes, he left me with three kids and no money. My sweet baby boy was in diapers, I had three children to feed. I don't how I endured that moment, but it was by God's grace! I had a little cash that my friend forced me to save for a rainy day. I had a couple of great friends that were cheering me on. They were great and gave me some great advice. Through the next months, I really was going to need their love and support. The money I put away was not enough to do much; I could buy a little food and diapers. On top of everything else, the check I wrote to get my kids gifts out of layaway bounced. Not again, not another Christmas going through this. Thank God for parents again because my kids enjoyed their gifts on Christmas morning.

I thought *I am at the worst now so what else could happen?* Well, the next morning I woke up to no water, no gas, and no lights. Yes, he had shut off everything. I could have never imagined he would close the accounts or do all this. I had released him. I rolled out the red carpet for him. He wanted this. Why retaliate? It was getting quite tough! All I could do was pray! Then things got really interesting. That "still small voice" told me to sell, sell, sell! So, I opened my garage and went into selling mode. I sold everything I did not need; I sold jewelry, clothes, kitchen gadgets, boots and his tools. Anything and everything. I stripped myself of the few things I like which made me feel humiliated through the whole day. All things considered, I did make enough money to pay the deposits to get everything turned back on, and have never had an issue since.

I did not realize every setback was preparing my comeback. I did not realize my "umph" was coming alive! I felt terribly stripped of pride! Have you ever felt naked in a room filled with people because they knew every awful detail about you? I was emotionally stripped and now the few possessions I had were gone. *What else would I have to lose? What other shame would I endure? What else would be stripped and removed from me?* Three kids, no money. I had to find a job which meant leaving my kids! My precious little girl was in kindergarten. She was so young and so impressionable. What a terrible time for all this to happen. My boys were age three, and twenty-two months old. I was so sad for my children. I wasn't even able to imagine what they would have to go through. I needed money, and I needed it quickly! That was when my friend told me to get my real estate license. I had not worked in years. How? When? How? But it sounded promising, plus I would be working with great with people. People often would tell me that I could sell anything! (They also said I could make poop look good! I guess it was a compliment.)

I followed my friend's advice and went to school to become a real estate agent. It was not easy, but by the grace of God I got help. Financial help, help with kids, emotional help. Thank God! I was determined so I went straight through all the classes I needed. It was 180 hours plus 30 hours to study for the exam. It was a lot of time and energy. I didn't get much sleep during that time, but I needed my license so I could work. I was still waiting on divorce papers to be served! Nothing yet! Oh, how I cried and cried, it was so overwhelming. *Why did I have to start over? Why did I have to be humiliated? Why did I have to give up being a stay-at-home mom when that was what I loved? Why? Why? Why?* I cried so hard during my math class the teacher said I could reschedule my class since my tuition was already paid. I could not even study or do any math, I was a mess. I could not remember anything they were saying. They knew I would fail. I knew I would fail. But God! I knew I needed to finish this class, I needed to get licensed. Well, I did it and I did it good. I passed! The teacher told me he was shocked because he thought I would fail.

I was finally a Realtor, and ready to make money...but it's commission only! Well again–God helped me through! My days consisted of crying, loving my kids, working long hours, driving a lot, open houses, taking pictures, lots of phone calls. I was tired! I wanted to be home. Did anyone care? But God was so good he placed me at the right real estate office. It was right in the heart of Sugar Land, Texas. It was a very busy office. I started selling, listing and making calls. But I was still so broken.

I finally had the means to pay my full-time nanny. She had been kind enough to accept room and board for compensation until I got on my feet financially. She was wonderful! She also came with two children. She had a little girl the same age as my youngest, and the oldest one was about to be a teenager who had disabilities and required close attention. We were two adults living in a house with five children. With a very busy home and I was so tired and stressed, I had no strength to pray. I was trying to paste my life together, paying bills, and addressing home maintenance issues and the yard work, too. There was so much to deal with! I felt like a total failure no matter how hard I worked.

Even in the midst of my shattering world, somehow, there was that "still small voice" deep inside telling me things would change and get better. I started feeling that

God was opening doors. I had my first home sale. Then my second, and my third home and just kept on selling houses. By God's grace, I was the rookie of the year my first year! I received a trophy, and yes, there was an award ceremony for me. It felt so good! But all this came with a lot of time away from home and my children. My car became my home.

I had a lot of work and was pulling it together, and God again told me it's time to take a step of faith. I sensed that it was time for me to move on and I felt like I needed to move forward with divorce. Yes, in scripture it says that God hates divorce, and He does. He hates anything that hurts his children. He also hates adultery and He was releasing me to move forward without that pain and torment in my life. I know most would say how could God say that, well He can! I wanted to try just one more time so I met with my estranged husband to let him know I would give him the opportunity if he wanted to come back. I stressed it was not for me but for the kids. I knew my daughter was very sad and I felt the need my boys had for a father at home. Well, he said nope. So, I went straight to my attorney and–yes I did it–I filed for divorce. Ironically, even though he was the one who constantly threatened, I was the one who served HIM the papers! Now please know, I don't condone divorce, or take it lightly. But it takes two to make a marriage just like it takes two to tango. If one does not want to dance, you can't tango alone. I put in a lot of prayer and thought into that decision. I know it is not for every couple who are having difficulties, but it was for us. So, the process started. I thought it would take forever, but it was quick. I thought he would fight for the children, but he did not. Instead of asking for custody of the kids, he asked for the coffee maker! Which I made sure he did not get! The divorce was fast and easy. It took three months after I filed to be finalized, he tried to hold me in contempt for selling his tools and boots and that is how we ended up in court. Really! Remember that garage sale? He was mad I sold all his stuff! But it was community property, so the judge was on my side. Then he brought up that I had kicked him out! Really! Remember the letter? Remember I gave him a choice? To my surprise, the judge finalized our divorce that day and it was OVER! I do not think she wanted to see him again in her courtroom. The judge said, "Raise your right hand," and we were divorced. It was quick and I was so thankful! I could not take any more emotionally. I could not go back again and hear him tell the court I was an awful mother, that my kids had no clothes, or that I would get my nails done before their needs. All lies! He would say this every time and I would just stand there in disbelief.

I was so overwhelmed after court that I couldn't even walk or drive. I sat and cried and cried, my knees were seriously shaking so badly they were knocking. It took more than an hour before I was able to drive. I was not shaken because of him, by then I was done with him. I was crying because my future and my children's future looked bleak. The divorce stated that I would have to send my kids to their father's house every other weekend and on Wednesday evenings. This would go on till they are 18 years old and it seemed like that would be forever. I have to spend holidays and birthdays sharing my children.

To make matters worse after the divorce, I sent my first payment on my home and it was returned to me. I was awarded the house in the divorce and my ex-husband had been ordered to make sure the payments were updated. But instead of doing that, he started the foreclosure process without my knowledge. He told the judge the mortgage payments were current, which was again the requirement for finalizing the divorce. Nope, I did not check with the mortgage company, totally my fault. He had stopped paying it and the letters were going to his new address. I called the mortgage company, and they reviewed the foreclosure paperwork. They realized I had not signed any of the papers that had been sent to us. He signed but not me! So, they had to reopen the file. Thank God they did. Yes, more pain, more strain, more work. I had to save my home, my children's home! What an ordeal! Massive paperwork, interviews with all kinds of people, writing letters, proving myself. Why did I have to prove myself to this mortgage company when it was not even my fault? But God worked out every detail for my good and I was able to stay in my home, thanks to the mortgage assistance program. Best of all, my payments were lowered to $250 a month for three years to help me get my life back. It came with a lot of penalties and interest added into my loan, but I had my home. My children had their home, I could finally breathe a little easier! Finally, something positive happened for me and my babies! That home was one of my biggest blessings. The

kids were able to go to great schools and it was worth double what I paid for it once I eventually sold it. I made money
despite all the added expense.

At one point, I held three jobs at one point so my children
could have what they needed. I was so exhausted. I really
did not have much of a 'me' life, but I knew my kids were
good! If you would have known me at that time you would
not have ever seen me broken or tired. I never showed my
pain, scars, or brokenness anymore. I just did not and could
not. I was so determined to succeed. I was determined to
keep moving forward. I kept my faith close, I made mistakes, but kept on moving! I still did not see how someone
would love this broken vessel again. I aged just from sheer
work. My body aged faster from never sleeping and being
worn out. I questioned inside, *Would anyone ever be interested in me? Could someone find me attractive? Could someone
love me? Love my kids? Love this body? Yikes!*

You prepare a table before me in the presence of my enemies. You anoint my head with oil; my cup overflows

PSALMS 23:5 (NIV)

I can do all this through him who gives me strength.

PHILIPPIANS 4:13 (NIV)

Now faith is confidence in what we hope for and assurance about what we do not see.

HEBREWS 11:1 (NIV)

"I have told you all this so that you may have peace in me. Here on earth you will have many trials and sorrows. But take heart, because I have overcome the world."

JOHN 16:33 (NLT)

CHAPTER EIGHT

Life After Divorce

Oh boy, dating! I was a mom of three and my body was not that of a twenty-year-old anymore. I was trying to figure out who would love me because whoever it was would have this instant family of four. Who could love my children like their own? I would have to trust that person with both myself and my children. It was so difficult to imagine a husband, but to imagine a father was even harder. Oh God, how do I confidently stand naked in front of my next husband? As a woman it was hard. We are so concerned with our looks and bodies. We don't stop to realize beauty is from the inside. We are perfectly and wonderfully made by our Creator. The rejection from my ex left an image of myself that I had to work on improving. I was thirty-two, working hard and extremely tired; I was not sure someone could love me. I was not sure I could love me. I felt old. You know the saying she looks like she has had a hard life? That was me! That was exactly what I was feeling. I did begin dating and quickly found that men were attracted to me even with children. I dated all kinds of men. It did not take long before I had my first date; it was with a very young man, twenty-eight years old. Well, I thought this was young at the time. I met him through my brother at a bank. Ironic! I knew he would never be the one and he was not father material, but it was nice to be noticed. I never introduced him or any of my boyfriends that came later to my children. I just did not see a purpose. I learned to country dance, I went to a symphony, I dated men with sports cars and big trucks. Some had long hair, some had short hair. I sold a house to one, I ate all kinds of food, I saw movies, and I had so many experiences. I learned very quickly that I was not comfortable with them having their own children. I just could not handle more kids. Mine had been through so much and I did not want to divide my time with them on others. They needed my full attention and love. I learned from each man and drew knowledge from each relationship, but never saw any as father material.

Things had changed as I had to look out for my children and not just my desires. It was hard because I wanted to be loved, I wanted to belong to someone, but it was not happening. I made a few mistakes and realized that marriage without intimacy does not work and intimacy without love does not either! In all this, God still loved me, protected me, forgave me, and looked out for me. I did not realize this was preparing me for something incredible. I started to realize all that God had placed in me; I was a strong woman, not so bad looking. I was not totally convinced yet with how I saw myself naked in front of a mirror, but that would eventually change. Looking back, I can see where my strengths came out and my determination worked. I was learning to have discernment; who was good for me and who was not. I was learning that I had some great qualities in me. I was learning that it was not just who I would love but who would love me, and that person must love my children. The pain was becoming gain, the scars became beauty marks, the stretch marks and changes in my body became a symbol of mom excellence. Things were changing in me and for me. I managed to take care of my family, myself, my business, my household.

God is so good and so merciful. He never leaves you or forsakes you. He makes your crooked places straight and the rough ones smooth. He protects and defends. He is God! I started having life after divorce. My hurts started going away and my scars slowly healed. I made it! I was single mom getting comfortable dating and putting myself out there. I wasn't thinking much about marriage at that point, but I knew I still wanted to remarry one day. I never imagined how well God was pruning me during this phase of my life. He was pulling out the bad weeds. In my case it was bags of weeds. He was growing the good seeds in me that were always there!

One thing I made sure of was that I was serving the Lord! I had my kids involved in church. On Wednesdays I would help serve in the children's choir class. All three of my kids attended. On Sundays all four of us would go! It was the right place to be, but it also brought sadness to me. Imagine how I felt seeing complete families every week. Moms and Dads together with their children. When I joined the church, they took family photos of new members to hang on the wall. Well, there was my picture, the four of us, with no father, among all the family pictures. It was painful but I was going to serve my God, trusting He would change that picture soon!

Weeping may endure for a night, but joy comes in the morning.

PSALMS 30:5 (AMPC)

The righteous cry out, and the Lord hears them; he delivers them from all their troubles. The Lord is close to the brokenhearted and saves those who are crushed in spirit.

PSALMS 34:17-18 (NIV)

"My Father! If it is possible, take this cup of suffering from me! Yet not what I want, but what you want."

MATTHEW 26:39 (GNT)

Then WOW Happened

Two years after the divorce and I was doing pretty good. Everything was working out. It was hard being a single mom of three working all the time, but we were good. I was happy, my kids had their home, and I was caring for them. I was bouncing between showing houses, volunteering in my children's school activities, picking up and dropping off the kids and a part-time job in a jewelry store. I was determined to work hard and just wait until God showed me what was next. I had adjusted to having a very full house. Between my live-in nanny and I, we had my kids who were seven, five and three, and her kids, who were three and fifteen, all living in one house. It was exhausting! The fifteen-year-old was sick and needed attention so sometimes it was tough. But we made it. I loved closing homes and receiving my commission. I would take my whole household out to dinner. Sometimes we would take a carriage ride downtown or something else that was special. My pride, my confidence, my inner beauty was growing! My bank account was growing! I was learning to love myself again.

Then WOW happened. I was not expecting it, could not predict it but... wow! I met him! The love of my life! I worked part-time selling diamonds for a jewelry store and the extra money really came in great for all the extras. I would get to work in the evening and wear this particular ring that I loved every day. I just loved that ring! I told myself that one day a wonderful, gorgeous, man with blue eyes who had never been married and never had kids would come around the corner and sweep me away! Of course, part of this was hallucination, and part was hope!

Your words are powerful, and God hears your prayers! Be specific! I learned that quickly. I was standing at work and there he came up to the jewelry counter. Yes, my prayers came to life and there he was, a young man with blue eyes, never married, no kids, and good looking. Just what I had prayed for. Understand that so many times I wanted to just quit this gig at night, but it was really helping with the little things I could buy for the kids. Plus, that "still small voice" kept telling me no, don't quit. I learned that sometimes we have to endure things, but God turns it around for our good. The path might seem unfair, it may seem crooked and rough, but God!

One day, I was standing behind the jewelry counter just working and minding my own business, and my younger brother, who was also working at the same department store came by with his friend Tracy he met on the shipping dock and introduced us. I said "hi" and that was about it I never gave it a second thought at that moment. He appeared younger, maybe twenty-seven or twenty-eight. He was a perfect gentleman.

A little background on Tracy. He was born in Lubbock, Texas, in 1973, the youngest of seven, all of them boys, except for a sister who was the oldest. He lived in the country and was a small-town boy. He loved country music, jeans, boots, always wore a cowboy hat, and we were totally opposites. He is a quiet gentleman; reserved and stoic! He is just like his dad. His dad raised him and did an excellent job! His mom was ill at the time I met her and did not live too many years after. But he was her heart! Tracy was so kind and caring with her. You know the saying a man who is good to his mother will make a great husband. He was extremely country and of course I was a total big city girl; I was in dresses and high heels, he wore jeans and boots. I had never seen boots like his before. They seemed really odd to me with bumps on them that matched his belt. Plus, they looked orange to me! Later I found out they were full quill ostrich—a very high-end material. Who knew?

At the time, my brother and sister-in-law were living with me. I was helping them out for a while. One night I decided to go dancing with my sister-in-law. I decided to valet park when we arrived at the party. Safety first! I left a ring in my ashtray so that it would not be lost or stolen. It was a ring from a prior short engagement and was the one thing left of value I had. After the party I got in the car and the ring was gone. It was the one thing I kept from selling all my jewelry because I figured I might need the money later for something else. I never did! Oh, I cried and cried. I got home and Tracy was at my house visiting my brother. Again, I just thought of him as a friend. He saw that I was upset and offered to look in my car again in search of the ring. How nice was that? The ring was nowhere in the car. I didn't find the ring, but something did happen. As he was looking, I noticed his forearm was sexy to me. No way! I'm just a single 34-year-old with feelings! Needs! He was my brother's friend. Then unbelievably he had my nanny make me coffee to comfort me. He brought it to me on the couch while I was sitting there feeling self-pity! The night ended and I went to bed and did not think much about what had happened but I liked being treated so nicely.

A few days went by and we saw each other at work. I really had no idea what was coming my way. My brother had an outing with some friends to see a boxing match. I was invited, so I thought why not? Per the divorce papers, my ex-husband had the children every other weekend, so I was usually alone on those weekends. We arrived at the home where they were watching the match. They had some food but I planned on waiting a while until I made myself a plate. Well, well! To my surprise there he was, the cowboy with a plate for me. Now this is strange! I was not sure what was going on, but I sure liked the attention. He sat down next to me, and his shoulder tapped mine. Oh help! It happened again—I had a weird sensation inside...I think they call it butterflies! Well, I was not expecting them from him! He was my brother's friend! He was too young, too country, too reserved, just not my type. He was in college and working part-time. No way! That would never work in a million years, so I thought. Later that night, we went to play pool where we kind of flirted and just had fun. We ended up having midnight breakfast and he paid. He was such a gentleman! Well, as it happened, we shared our first kiss. Well, I kind of kissed him first! (Blushing!) We headed back to my house and of course he was still the perfect gentleman and he walked me to the door. Okay, before the door! He leaned over in his little red sports car and kissed me. Now, he asked first! It was totally sexy that he asked. We kissed, then kissed, and maybe one more kiss!

Obviously, our relationship changed just a bit after that. Next time we went out we went again with my brother and his wife to the Big Monster Truck Show. Such intriguing dates! Thank God my dear brother kept persisting that I go out with all of them. I figured things were getting serious because he bought me a balloon that said I LOVE YOU! Again, bam! I love romance! The next date we had, which was about our fourth date, we had the kids with us. Oh boy, my kids are busy and quite rambunctious. I was praying he would not run away! He decided to rent videos, the way we used to do it, and bring pizza over. He was an instant hit. My three loved him. They initiated him by jumping and climbing on him all evening, but he seemed content. I was content. It was the first feeling of being a complete family in a long time!

So just to recap, a week after we met, we were talking, a week later we were dating, a week later he told me he loved me, and a week later that ring was on my finger! Thirty days later we were married!

I loved that Tracy bonded with my kids like crazy! In fact, they bonded so well they all had chicken pox two weeks before the wedding! Thank God they all cleared up in time for the wedding. Yes, that was quick! Now I don't advise this for everyone, but for me it was like a Hallmark movie; my favorite one to this day. We were in love like crazy and he wanted to take care of me, my children, my home. I was like how could that work? He was young and still in school. But he was different. Kind, gentle, loving, respectful. Oh, but young! Yes, thirteen years younger. A little younger than I had thought. He was twenty-one and I was thirty-four. Cougar! Yes, me a cougar! I had not thought of that one, but God does have a sense of humor! Yikes! I lived in a 34-year-old body after having three kids. Help! So now how do I love myself naked and with him? Imagine at twenty-one he could have picked a young chick, but he picked me. He told me he had asked God to make his choice clear when he met his future wife. I loved that about him, he knew who God had sent and stayed the course in making it happen. We worked together as I had mentioned and there were so many young girls his age. I would hear them talking to each other about trying get his attention and going on a date with him. No one knew we were dating. It all happened so fast. He had not dated since high school and did not run around, if you know what I mean. So, he was ready to fall in love. Then the day came when he asked me to marry him in front of the whole store and purchased the ring. Yes, the ring that I would always wear while working. I would wear it and dream of that day. Remember my rings I had to sell so that I could provide for my kids? Restored! God! God! God! All this was awesome. The craziest part was all the young pretty girls that I worked with were all hoping for a date with him and so they were shocked! YES ,YES, YES! I got the prize. It felt good to know I still had it! Well, we got married month later and it was a beautiful wedding. That was almost 27 years ago. It was in a small barn church; an intimate fairytale. Those doors opened, and I walked down the aisle behind my three incredible kids and met my destiny at the altar. I had thought about all the things that could go wrong, but that "still small voice" said let yourself go, fall in love with this one, get married. I listened this time!

Thank God I have come a long way in listening to Him! My husband gently showed me how beautiful I am to him. He spoke, and still speaks words of kindness to me every day. He loved my children as his own, and provided for them, and we were so thankful. After the wedding, he suggested that I should quit my part-time job and to do real estate as much as I wanted or not wanted. He told me our kids needed me. Dinners at the table as a family, and all the things my kids deserve. What a man, what a dad! Again, thank God he restored my family. He decided to work full time and quit college. He is the best at what he does and now owns his own private investigation and security business. I was restored as a full-time mom! Amen! I was going to get to be nacho mom, pizza mom, dance mom, football mom, ROTC (Reserve Officers Training Core) mom and just mom with him next to me at everything. God does give us double for our trouble. His promises are yes and amen!

I literally felt like Cinderella on my wedding night and the honeymoon was fantastic. We stayed at a hotel in town. We did not want to be far from the kids and funds were tight. We never left the room! Awwwww! My Hallmark story begins! All this was awesome. Before, I had felt ashamed, exposed, sad, depressed. Now God turned it around! I was picked to be his bride. I was proud, happy, excited, chosen! No more ugly nakedness; I was covered by love! Things were great and we just bonded, all five of us. But of course, as a woman, I could see the physical changes and aging process and who enjoys that? The years passed so quickly; we were so happy and enjoyed our lives.

As time went by, I noticed I had started aging. Bummer, just as things were going so well, I was getting older, reaching my forties, and trying literally to like myself naked. Like literally in a mirror. I hated those dressing room mirrors! So, my new little journey started, how to get older physically with a younger mind, and trying to love that forty-something naked me! Always something!

Even to your old age and gray hairs I am he, I am he who will sustain you.

ISAIAH 46:4 (NIV)

Therefore we do not lose heart. Though outwardly we are wasting away, yet inwardly we are being renewed day by day.

2 CORINTHIANS 4:16 (NIV)

The righteous will flourish like a palm tree, they will grow like a cedar of Lebanon; planted in the house of the Lord, they will flourish in the courts of our God. They will still bear fruit in old age, they stay fresh and green...

PSALMS 92:12-14 (NIV)

CHAPTER TEN

Beginning To Heal

We go through a lot, and we learn a lot. Some good, some not so good, but we learn from it. Challenges are always there, just different in nature. I had to learn to love me again to be able to accept the outer shell as it matured, and the inner one that had been so broken. It took a lot of courage to undress and be sexy, but I did it. I started pressing into God's word where he reminded me that He loved me, that I was amazing, I am wonderfully made, I am His masterpiece. I needed to understand that my husband loved me so much that the changes did not matter. Now this took time, but every loving word, every sweet caress made it easier. But I needed God's peace because those darn recordings in my head would remind me of what had happened. At that time, I was young and lean, what about now? I am not. I discovered that my walk with the Lord was also changing.

I have always loved Jesus and always have trusted him, but age does bring wisdom and an urgency to have a closer walk with God! My husband and I had so much fun as parents and partners. That honeymoon in town was followed up with lots of travel. Cruises, Hawaii, Alaska, Disney and so much more. I'm not bragging on myself; I'm bragging on my God! He does turn your ashes into beauty! We stood beside each child as they danced, played basketball, participated in ROTC. We wore our Mommy and Daddy T-shirts with pride as we stood side by side watching each of their accomplishments. He took tons of pictures and videos and still does. Drives me crazy, but I love all the memories that he captures! So many memories. We celebrated birthdays and accomplishments and felt our kids' heartaches together. We taught them how to bicycle and how to drive. Phones, cars, pick them up, drop them off, proms, homecomings, friends. We were so busy. I am sure many can relate to this. We just needed God's help, endurance, and provisions.

We served God and made sure our kids were in church. We never had children together. I asked but he said he would never make me go through anything that could harm me. He told me we had three kids and that was great! Gentle words, loving words. The type of words that heal. Now it was not all so easy. Each child had to go through adjustments. I remember the nights my middle child, my son, would scream and scream. My youngest son developed an eye blink that drove me crazy, but it finally went away. My daughter would vomit, yes vomit. Every time I would leave my daughter at school, she would make herself vomit so they would call me back to the school. She suffered so much separation anxiety. All of this happened when they were very young. When we married, they were seven, five and four. I could not leave their sight, especially at school. Sometimes I had to stay in a class or sit at a school for a while before I could leave. Yes, this too came to pass. The doctor explained that it was normal after so much had occurred. Thank God, He healed all three.

But then as life would have it, I fell sick. I held so much in for so long. I woke up one early morning, my heart was pounding, my hands were sweating, I thought I was having a heart attack. We called 911 and they rushed me to the hospital. I found out it was an anxiety attack. For those who have suffered them or still have them, they are real and scary. I empathize with you because I understand the tremendous time this takes from your life. There is no fast cure, and the doctors think you are crazy! I continued having anxiety attacks for two years with many hospital visits. One Fourth of July, I went to the ER four times. It was bad, but God could heal this! I prayed, prayed, and prayed.

Fortunately, circumstances were better in my life, however my past was catching up with me. I had no idea what backlash was, and it was haunting me when I was finally my happiest. Doctors tried giving me medication but no way! I hate medication and surely did not want anything that was addicting. I sat and asked God to heal me and I would remind Him of His word and His promises. I would shout out, "I am healed in the name of Jesus! By his stripes I am healed!"(Isaiah 53:5). Sometimes I would yell while having a panic attack. I would walk for miles and sometimes throughout the night to help ease the panic attack. I was exhausted, but I kept up the good fight. I fought my battle with God at my side. The devil wants to attack us, especially when we are walking into our divine destination. Jeremiah 17:14 says, "Heal me Lord, and I will be healed!" Jeremiah 30:17 says, "I will give you back your health, and heal your wounds, says the Lord." I stood firm on His word and one day I was healed. My husband stood by me, prayed with me and he was a great dad during this time.

As my children aged, we went through so much. My daughter had her first broken heart, both of my sons did too. They all graduated and you would think it would get easier. But as I said changes kept coming but God was still on the throne. All three were working hard, two were in college, one was moving up quickly at his job. Then my future son-in-law came into the picture, but we didn't know it at the time. He was a friend of my son's but he was also a bully and had nowhere to stay so yes, I took him in. He did not have the same Christian background we had. I said he could stay two weeks...which turned into four years. It was rough. It took years to peel off the rough exterior but under all that there was a big teddy bear heart. I spent my time taking him to work, helping him get his license, treating him just like my own son. Then what happens? He falls in love with my daughter. She fell in love too, and wouldn't listen to me telling her "No, no, no! Not this man!" He turned his life around, went to school, got a great job and best of all, he dedicated his life to Christ. As the years past they, of course, finally decided on marriage. Now when I say finally, I mean finally. It took about eight years. I became his mom, and since his dad had nothing to do with him, Tracy was like his only dad. We didn't mind because by this time we all had fallen in love with him too!

Around the same time, my oldest son met Whitney, a past girlfriend from high school, and rekindled their love. Before I knew it, I had two married children! I was so proud of my son and his choice. She is strong and loving. Beautiful inside and out. She is a great match and makes him happy. We get along with her sweet parents and now things were going great! Now my third child, my son, well he takes a whole chapter. He was doing great, got through high school and then things shifted. He was in college getting close to finishing, when things went very wrong. The kind of wrong that keeps a mom on her knees crying out to heaven, raw and undone. Worst kind of nakedness! Raw emotions that only God can repair and restore.

"Behold, I am the Lord, the God of all flesh; is there any-thing too difficult for Me?"

JEREMIAH 32:27 (AMP)

Beloved, do not be surprised at the fiery ordeal among you, which comes upon you for your testing, as though some strange thing were happening to you; but to the degree that you share the sufferings of Christ, keep on rejoicing, so that also at the revelation of His glory you may rejoice with exultation.

1 PETER 4:12-13 (NASB1995)

Be strong and courageous, do not be afraid or tremble at them, for the Lord your God is the one who goes with you. He will not fail you or forsake you.

DEUTERONOMY 31:6 (NASB1995)

"I will give you back your health and heal your wounds," says the Lord.

JEREMIAH 30:17 (NLT)

My Baby, Joshua

Psalms 23 says, *Though I walk through the valley of the shadow and death I will fear no evil. Thy rod, thy staff comfort me!* It's one thing to walk in the valley. It's another thing to see your kids walk through the valley. There is no pain like your kids' pain. I just want to take on their suffering and endure it for them. Now I tried, but God reminded me one day that He was God, not me. He said, *When you are ready to step back and give Me My space to handle all this I will.* But that is hard. We pray and place it on His throne of grace and then we pick it right back up and try to figure it all out.

Let me start with my youngest, my baby, Joshua. They always stay the baby. I tease him now that he has the longest chapter in my book! He decided to get a degree in philosophy. Now there is nothing wrong with that...until you start believing all the crap they are teaching. Can I say "crap"? Looks like I just did. Add to that drugs and drinking and it becomes a nightmare. That led to confused gender choices. Now this is very personal, but I do believe that God gives us our valleys to use as testimonies. What good is it to hold all these testimonies inside of me? I hope it will help some parents out there. I could never even imagine all that was going to happen. Thank God for holding my child in His hands and giving me strength. He was slowly spiraling down; he believed all the teachers spoke about God in a way that was not of the Bible. He used all the drugs that he could get. Weed was the start, but it was a gateway to cocaine and other drugs. Finally, he just quit school in his Junior year of college. One day he showed up about 2:00 a.m. at my house. He came home scared and shaking. He told me that people were following him to hurt him. Of course, I panicked, but no one came. He told me how the birds and animals follow him and that he was the Trinity–the Godhead: Father, Son, and Holy Spirit.

At this point I didn't know what to do. I was praying and had a great need for God to show up. But as we know it, His timing is not ours, and His ways are not our own. My son was so out of his mind that he was convinced I was not even his mother. I thought I had felt the worst pain possible previously in my life, but this made everything I went through seem nice. The hurt was horrible. He lived with us, but it was a very hard. He was not the child I raised anymore or even knew. He would say crazy awful things and I would just pray, sometimes I would just scream! He couldn't keep to the rule of no drugs while living under our roof. He was in and out of our house, living here and there. Then came my worst nightmare. He became disrespectful and just out of his mind, so he had to move out. He lived in his car. I could have fallen apart, but God's grace carried me through this too! He had no job because he couldn't hold one down. No money, no food, no baths, and gender confusion. I paid for his phone so we could communicate. Even as I am writing this, I have tears running down my face. I know moms understand my feelings. He had everything and the drugs were stealing his whole life in front of me.

The devil steals and destroys! I scolded and punished and preached but nothing mattered to him. On his twenty-sixth birthday, we met for dinner, this is the second year dealing with all this. He was still living in his car and still would tell me I was not his mother. I finally decided to give up; I had to give it up to God. I could not handle this, it was too serious, and my child was in danger. I just could not go on. So, I kissed him and knew I would not see him again for a while. I told God that night to do whatever he needed to wake up my son and change his life; anything short of him or someone else killing him. It was very hard because I knew God *would* do what was needed and I really had no idea what to expect. That's where the trust comes in; we have to lean into God with all we have. We have to acknowledge that He is good and loves us. I knew He loved my son more than I could. I knew He had more resources than I did. I knew He had a way and I did not!

As I prayed, it happened. One night after church on a Wednesday, we had just worshiped and served, and the hit came. We got an awful call. Our son had just been arrested. He was in a drug psychosis and was caught for theft in a store. I just fell to my knees and cried and cried and cried. My baby was in jail and out of his mind. Why? Why? Then

God spoke, yes, the Holy Spirit is that " still small voice" I often heard, and he reminded me that I had asked for God to do something without my son getting hurt so now I just needed to trust God. Wow. He is right, I did pray that. The trust kicked in, the pain was still there, the sadness and disappointments were there, but I believed in my God. I believed in His mighty hand and His mighty works.

The hard part was after the call, it was like silence. Every time I would call the jail, they would tell me he was an adult, and I had no rights to any information. You are kidding! He was my baby! This is where I know there is a God, and you will soon see how He shows up in so many ways. One day, I called the jail and had no idea that my son hadn't signed a release form to allow anyone to talk to me about his condition. I found this out from a kind gentleman on the phone. The man told me that my son was being held in a mental health section of the jail. I was not sure why that was so comforting, but it was. He told me about video visits and commissary deposits. We deposited money so he could get some goodies on a daily basis. I didn't care where my child was, I had to help some way. I could not talk to him, so I paid for my first video visit. Yes, pay! I waited for that day and time. It had been a few weeks and I had no contact with him. It was the first time ever in his life that I went more than a day without talking to him. I was on my phone waiting for him to pop on. I waited, I waited and waited. I cried. I screamed at my phone, I yelled, "help me Lord", but nothing. The allotted time had passed. No son, no face. I was so hurt. It was so painful! I tried two or three more times and nothing. I did not realize he just wasn't in his right mind and that he had no idea I was waiting.

When I would call the jail, the words "WAITING FOR IN-MATE" would appear on the phone. I would sit for the fifteen minutes allowed and wait. For the first few times, my son never would pick up so the call would end after I waited the fifteen minutes. Then one day, the words changed to "INMATE JOINING." It was a bit scary, but those words were beautiful to me at that moment. There he was, my child, my baby, my heart! He finally picked up the video phone call. I did not know what to say. He was not coherent, and that was so sad. He said again that I was not his mom, but he talked about the goodies, and I was happy he had them. It was hit and miss the next few video messages and he responded the same, no changes. But each time we spoke he was eating cookies, candy, or chips that he bought with the commissary money. For me as a mom, any glimmer of love that I could give him gave me hope! One day, I called again trying to get information. It was not easy because sometimes the staff could be a bit abrupt, but I was persistent. I explained that my son was not even capable of coming each time to the video appointments. How did they expect me to just wait and wait with no idea what was happening? He told me they would be moving him soon. He would be going to a mental health facility, but I would not know where or when. I was desperate by then. I had just finally found him and worked all the details out at that location. The man on the phone could not say much more because my son was an adult and still had not signed any releases for me to get information. He just wasn't in his right mind to sign any papers. I told one of the staff members on the phone how I prayed for my son, and would continue and that people at my church were praying. I said there were a lot of people praying because at the time I went to Lakewood in Houston. "Oh my!" he said, "I used to go there till I got this job that moved me." Okay God, go! We began talking about the church and God and the conversation just shifted. The next thing I knew, my son signed the release, and I was able to have contact and get information. So, the day came when I called, and he was not there because he had been moved. My contact was not in that day of course. But he had told me they would probably move him to Vernon, Texas. Wow! So far from Houston.

I prayed hard that I would find him soon since a new release would have to be signed at the new facility. A couple of days went by, and I got antsy, but I had no choice but to wait to hear from him again. Oh, how I prayed. The nights were so long just knowing he was somewhere ugly and dark, with no goodies. One day, I was in the car and a call came through from Conroe, Texas, which was about an hour from my house. I picked it up and I heard my son's voice. I tried to ask him questions, but we lost our call, and he did not call back. But I saw Conroe on my phone, and I believed in a miracle. My sweet husband, who can find anything because he is so smart, found a facility in Conroe that was a mental rehab place. (I guess that Eagle Scout and PI training kicked in on my husband.) He found out we could go on weekends and check if my son was there. The next Saturday I was ready. My stomach hurt and I was so nervous, but God! The ride seemed to take forever, but we arrived. My husband and I boldly walked in and asked for my son. They took our licenses and moved us to a waiting area. Oh my God, I was going to get to see him. Oh my God, I will get to hug him! I will get to kiss him and tell him how much I loved him. We were then escorted to a large room with lots of people, tables, and a very friendly atmosphere. I was so glad to see how nice the facility was. The employees were so friendly and very clean. It had many windows, and I was very comforted. I looked over at a table and there he was – my son! My heart! I was elated. I cried and cried. We hugged and we kissed. He was still confused, but I did not care because he was in my arms. We spent the day with him and ordered lunch to be delivered, which was also so nice. I was thankful he was close to home, and I could see him every Saturday and Sunday from 9 a.m. to 3 p.m. and I did! About three months had passed since I had hugged him and it was hard, but God started the healing process. It might not seem that way in the natural, but God works in the supernatural! The weeks passed, and my son went up and down... I was thankful for the ups. I prayed for supernatural healing, protection, good people around him. One day he called, and he said, "Hello Mommy." I was shocked – his voice was that of my son's. He acknowledged me as his mom. From that point on he called every day all day. I mean all day, but I was totally content with that. We would see him, and we enjoyed our weekend visits. We laughed and prayed. He would just sit for hours holding my hand.

All the employees told me he was going to be fine, and he would be the one to finish college, work and be all I prayed he would be. They said he would be one of the small statistics that make it! So sad, but I was thrilled they saw in him what I could not see yet. The staff were listening to my prayers that I said while I sat with him, and they spoke hope into me. They would open a little office so we could hold hands and pray. Boy did we pray. I am sure the whole room heard, and some others were blessed, I found out later. The courts had to deem him incompetent to place him there in the first place. I remember that moment and I was overwhelmed. But the day came when he was tested and deemed competent! Hallelujah Jesus! Prayers were being answered. Now it was time for him to move back to the original jail and out of the mental facility. I told him to call me first thing in the morning and last thing at night. This was my way of knowing he was still in the same facility. Unfortunately, the mental facility could not let me know he was being transferred out. My only notification was the day I did not hear from him. I knew he was moved back to the regular jail. That day came. There was no longer a safe zone where I could visit him or call him. Did I mention... but God! I called my son's lawyer and he said he would check on him and call me back. He called me back and asked if I wanted to pick up my son. Yes! Yes! When? He told me to head to the jail immediately. I was about three hours away and did not even stop. I kept on driving and headed to where my son was placed in jail. I had a car full of people–my daughter, my mother, and grandson–and we just took off and got there fast. The lawyer said it could take hours and maybe go into the morning for his release papers to be issued so I could pick him up. But, I was ready to see him. I would wait for however long it took. I parked in front of the exit door of the jail and I was not about to move. It was taking a while and I was getting concerned but there was no way I leave that spot. My son called and said, "Mom, I want to get out, I am ready."

"It will be soon, we are just waiting on your release papers."

He was anxious to get out of there and I felt the same way. I told him I wanted to pray over him, for peace and patience and for me, too! I prayed that God would move the hand of the person who was doing his release. That they would release him right then! When I was done praying, I started to talk to him but there was no response. I was thinking, where did he go? Why is he not responding on the phone? I wanted him to call again please! This was happening about an hour after we arrived at the jail, and they had said it could take hours, or possibly until the next morning. Then this strange number came up and I answered and yes! My son! Those three sweet words came out of his mouth: "I'm coming out!" Yes, God's promise fulfilled! What a reunion at that door. What a blessing, what a gift from God! Well, short story, ha ha, he came home! There were a couple of small adjustments, but they were minor. We had two great years. He started working, finishing his college classes, driving, and knowing who his mom is. Most importantly he knew who his God was and how big He was. My prayers daily were that he would come out of this not even smelling like smoke. My Shadrach, Meshach, and Abednego testimonial (Daniel 3 NIV). That was what I prayed for; that is what my God did!

I remember sitting at church and I had my phone with my son on the line while he was in the mental facility so he could hear the music and the sermon. It was so clear to me that God was in control when pastor mentioned Shadrach, Meshack and Abednego, and how they didn't even smell like smoke! Still small voice again, Holy Spirit! This was a great move of God!

Mental illness is not easy for a family. Joshua has had some relapses due to refusing his meds and episodes. We went two years on medication prescribed and it was great. I am still not sure at times on his future or if I am equipped to handle his moods, but one thing I know for sure is that God did it once and brought him out great and he will continue to take care of him forever! There are so many side effects to his medications. One of the major ones is Tardive Dyskinesia which is uncontrolled muscle spasms in the face. His back has bowed and it's difficult to walk that way. It also causes him to choke at times while eating. This is a terrible condition, and it breaks my heart to see him go through this. But I am determined to stay on course and continue to pray, hope, and love! Above all, this momma is thankful to have her son back and he is doing well.

Let us then approach God's throne of grace with confidence, so that we may receive mercy and find grace to help us in our time of need.

HEBREWS 4:16 (NIV)

And after you have suffered a little while, the God of all grace, who has called you to his eternal glory in Christ, will himself restore, confirm, strengthen, and establish you.

1 PETER 5:10 (ESV)

"Come to me, all you who are weary and burdened, and I will give you rest."

MATTHEW 11:28 (NIV)

My Beautiful Daughter

I was so devastated about my son, but in the midst of the struggle I found out I was going to be a "Gami!" My dream, my hope, the one thing I could not wait for, and I waited a long time! My daughter, Monique, called to tell me she was pregnant. We were so excited. Then it was time to wait on the gender. It seemed like forever. A few weeks later, Monique wanted to meet me at the store. She greeted me with an "It's a Boy" balloon. I was in love and told her that I was going shopping! I always wanted it to be a little girl, but when I found out it was a boy, I was like, "Who needs a girl?" The baby nursery was beautiful and the shower was great. We would listen to the heartbeat every day! Sometimes over the phone she'd let me hear the heartbeat if I was not with her. Finally! I was elated. The pregnancy was good; the labor, not so good. My daughter had an unexpected C-section. It was tough, but they both came out of it fine. This wonderful baby boy was here, they named him Luke. I can't even find a word to describe my feelings. I just knew I wanted the best for him. He had good hard-working parents, a nice home, grandparents that would spoil him, and so much more to look forward too.

Luke was born about the time Joshua went to Conroe for therapy. It was a tough time, but I was a "Gami!" When we got the baby home, Tracy and I helped my daughter tote everything into her home. We were busy trying to put bottles, diapers, car seat, stroller and all that stuff up. It had been so long since I had a baby, I was occupied trying to figure out all the new gadgets that I did not have for my kids. My daughter came over to me and whispered, "I don't think we are gonna make it."

"Sure you will." I said.

"No." She replied.

I didn't know what she was talking about.

"We can help you financially if you need it." I said, trying to offer help. But then she said something that really shocked me.

"Mom, he doesn't want to be my husband anymore. He doesn't want to be a daddy."

I was speechless.

But just for a moment. I had plenty to say...and I said it. The emotions I felt in that moment were raw and hurt, like someone had just stabbed my heart–and the heart of my precious daughter. We knew he had a moment earlier on in her pregnancy when he was nervous about becoming a dad. His own dad left when he was a baby and that hurt him deeply growing up, so we knew he was a little concerned.

He had no example of fatherhood, but never realized it was that serious. This beautiful gift I waited so long for— my grandbaby–was going to be put through this. In my greatest moment I had to suffer my greatest pain.

Oh, this pain was awful. The thought of my grandson suffering was more than I wanted to take on. I knew my grandson would suffer without his dad at home. I knew the pain kids felt because I lived it with my children. We cried and we cried. Me, my hubby and my daughter spent night after night feeding, singing, holding this amazing gift while his father was gone. He immediately started going out and had other women. My daughter had not even healed yet. Hubby and I, at our age, became co-parents. We never intended that to happen, but it did. Everything changed so fast. Sometimes we just don't understand why, but God gives us the endurance to run the race. It had been years since I had stayed up all night and my husband soon found out how to work with no sleep. My daughter was on an emotional roller coaster and had to go back to work earlier than we thought. I put my businesses on hold to take care of my grandbaby full time. My daughter was now alone in her home, so we spent a lot of time going back and forth to be with her. All we knew was that we were in love with this baby. We would spend hours watching him sleep. Mesmerized is the word. So cute and cuddly, how could you just walk away? But his father did. This man, who we took in, gave him everything we could, loved him like our son, and he just bolted. Everything in my daughter's life caved in. He lost his job, and she was stuck trying to figure out the bills all alone. He caused her so much pain. There was nothing we could do but watch and hurt and pray! I wish I had a happy ending, but unfortunately, I don't when it comes to him. He didn't want the responsibility of the baby, the house, the bills. So, this was a massive burden on her. We felt so sad because she had worked so hard, loved her home and was a good wife. We helped her as much as we could financially so she could keep her house and have food on the table. We prayed and hoped every day and trusted that God would work things out.

The pain I suffered in my life wasn't anything compared to the pain of watching my daughter suffer with my grandson. The valleys taught me what I needed to do to get through this. My husband was amazing. He had never experienced taking care of a baby, so he was enjoying it. The months passed and I watched my daughter's pain go up and down. Finally, she said, "Mom, I'm coming home. I'm done. He has put me through enough." This took two years and a lot of tears. I was so comforted in knowing they would be with us. Nothing like a full home! We lost some of the sweet times we should have had because we were disgusted with the situation, but we survived. Many nights of no sleep but also much laughter over everything my grandbaby did and does even today. I am not sure what her future holds but I'm sure it's good. I am sure God will give her double for her trouble. She has healed emotionally and is so happy with her son! One day God will give her a new home, a great husband, and a fantastic daddy for her son. The Lord will restore everything! She is now so happy and comfortable with herself. Monique is raising her son and making sure he goes to church. I'm so proud of her! Who knows, maybe she will write a book one day. And I am totally confident that my grandson will be amazing!

As a mother, I hated what my daughter's husband did to her and my grand-baby, and sometimes I hated him. The fact that he hurt my daughter so much was overwhelming and then he wasn't present very much the first year of my grandson's life. When I did see him, he always had some smart remark and I had to bite my tongue (and to be truthful, it's not easy for me). I am a woman of much advice and opinions. There were times of screaming, and the occasional cuss word that I thought he needed. Mostly, I would talk and try to be a civilized Christian woman. As time goes by, we have to find a way to deal with the situation. We understand he will be part of our lives forever. I do love him and pray for him each day and though it has become easier, and I have become stronger, there still are those moments! It's never easy sharing your children or grandchildren with the one who brought the pain!

Get rid of all bitterness, rage and anger, brawling and slander, along with every form of malice.

EPHESIANS 4:31 (NIV)

Fools give full vent to their rage, but the wise bring calm in the end.

PROVERBS 29:11 (NIV)

A soft answer turns away wrath, but a harsh word stirs up anger.

PROVERBS 15:1 (ESV)

My Handsome Son!

My middle son is so handsome. Nathan looks like a movie star. He has the new long beard thing going on, but I still love him. He is very quiet and reserved, which is a contrast to my other two children and myself. He acquired a little bit of Tracy's personality; he's the strong, silent type and full of integrity. I am so thankful for that. He is the one who always gets promoted quickly and he is so helpful. He is the man of the house and is proud to take care of his wife and child. He is so different from the other two loud ones! He suffered from heartache early on but nothing too major. He was a lady's man, so he had no problems with girlfriends. One day I saw him with a girl, and I remembered who she was. They had dated before. I thought she was crazy when she dated him in high school. She would just sit forever watching him play basketball! I'm like, "Girl you need to move on!" But then she showed up many years later. Obviously, they still cared for one another which then grew into love. We planned a beautiful wedding for them and enjoyed every moment of it. Our families get along great, and

I am so blessed for that. They married and bought a lovely home. They make a beautiful couple and seem very happy!

Soon after the wedding they wanted children. They surprised me with a card that stated I was going to be a Gami again. I was ready! I just love me some more grandbabies. That would put the babies about four months apart. Two babies, how wonderful! I was so honored when they let me go to the first doctor's visit. The heartbeat was a little slow, but we were excited about the baby. Two weeks later, we went back for a check-up and the baby's heartbeat could not be heard. Oh, no, no! The baby's heart had stopped. Instant pain! I just hate when my children hurt. As a mom, we want to make it right for them and in some cases we just can't. This all happened the day after my youngest son, Joshua, got arrested and placed in jail. No Lord, too much, too fast. I remember being on the phone with the jail and trying to get information while walking into the doctor's office with my other son and daughter-in-law. Though my daughter had not had her baby yet, she was going through a little rough patch with her husband and was having some reservations about their marriage. We just pushed it off that he was nervous about the baby. So, all three of my children were at the same time dealing with big situations. Until God shows me later how much bigger He is compared to my problems. I was exhausted, sad, and lost. I was hurting for my son and his wife. Sad for my daughter and her son. Sad about losing my grandchild and wondering if there was enough grace? But yes, there is! Grace, grace, powerful grace! A few months later, my daughter-in-law was pregnant again. This was difficult! Momma was concerned with each week that passed just praying this pregnancy would be good. I spent the same time just praying and being thankful for every week that she progressed. That second pregnancy was wonderful! We had a gender reveal and yes, a boy! I was so happy. She had a quick labor with absolutely no complications. My second wonderful grandson was born, my sweet Nate. God is so good all the time. We worry and we need not to! God is in control and has every moment of our life planned. Now I have two out-of-this-world gorgeous grandsons, Luke and Nate! My two little joys! They are 51 weeks apart, both born in February. We are busy in February! At this present time, my youngest is out of rehabilitation and doing good, my daughter is enjoying her life again, my middle son and his wife have settled into parenting with our new grandson Noah, after going through a second miscarriage. My daughter-in-law decided to become a housewife and so everything is good. We are enjoying grandparenting and are thankful that God is so good!

Take delight in the Lord, and he will give you the desires of your heart.

PSALMS 37:4 (NIV)

Do not be anxious about anything, but in every situation, by prayer and petition, with thanksgiving, present your requests to God.

PHILIPPIANS 4:6 (NIV)

Evolving Me

I can't even begin to explain the toll that all of the challenges of life take on the mind and body. My husband and I have been juggling for a while now and we need rest! I'm noticing the frown lines are more apparent, the little spider veins, the skin changes, the gray that I can't even keep covered anymore. I am a Gami and proud, but who wants to look like one? Sometimes in life we just have no time for ourselves. Life passes by and we haven't been aware of the physical changes. We definitely feel the changes, but we're not in tune with all that is happening or why. Though I am strong and courageous; I am starting to take notice of myself. My nakedness is yuck!

Well, I think so! Ask my husband and he would have a different opinion. It is not easy growing old, especially when it happens so fast with so many struggles that age you. When worry, anxiety, and stress makes a home in this human body of ours, I am here to say, stop! We have one life. Yes, there will be difficulties, but learn to release them to God! We allow so much trash into our mind and we let fear and worry rob us of joy! It also robs your face and body and health. I know women struggle and we don't get much help in this area. Society is inundated with what women should look like: thin, chesty, long hair, big injected lips. Everywhere you look, you see it in magazines, billboards, TV, and the internet. We are bombarded by images of what we should look like. How about the fifty-something grandma who sacrifices and fights hard for her family and has no time for fixing herself up? The young twenty-five-year-old with two kids and a job who has zero time to take care of herself? The forty-year-old who is sick and struggling and can't take care of her body? Maybe you don't have the money for all the glamour. How about menopause? How do I survive it?! How do I deal with it? Changes! This is a tough time for women. On one hand, there is no more monthly cycle. Woo hoo! On the other hand, hormones are going dormant! Dry skin, dry everything, body shifting, hot flashes, tired, no energy, anxiety, hormones are driving you nuts. Help me now, I need to crawl out of my own body! I blink and I have arrived on the other end of life. I get discounts for seniors now and they don't ask for my ID.

What happened? No one asked me if this was okay! God help me love this woman. Help me feel pretty, accepted, confident. Help me feel sexy. I'm still married, I still want romance, I still want to have fun! So now I stand in front of the mirror, and I have to live it in this new body. How? I remember that God loves me. I have to remember that He made me just as I am. I am His masterpiece. I am a child of the Most High God! I am beautiful in His eyes! God loves me! I am blessed to be healthy and strong! I am not sure what challenge you are facing. Maybe you are in your twenties and just finished college, or about to get married, or have your first real job, or maybe your first child. Maybe you're in your thirties: married, children, home, a little more strapped of money. How about those forties: teenagers, single mom maybe or married but too busy for each other, starting to feel the early signs of perimenopause but not sure what it is. You're just up and down, a bit tired and frustrated. Or maybe you're in those fifties: children should be all grown up but not totally... well they never really grow up. Exhausted, menopause is causing you to pull out your hair, you can lose hair easily at this point, you're nauseous sometimes, your skin is dry, all your skin and face products are not agreeing with you anymore. You're looking for things that include collagen, vitamin A, hyaluronic acid, anything that says it will help you age gracefully or remove those new fine lines. Sex is getting a little tougher, you're just too tired or hormones are all over the place. Maybe sixties: The weight just isn't coming off like before, no face and skin products work. We dress different, we are treated different. It's a bunch of ma'am in my life now and everywhere I go, I get the senior discounts automatically. I am not close to seventy yet, but my friends that are encourage me by reminding me that by then, you are just happy to be alive and healthy. You get past trying to look young and then you're okay with looking at the younger crowd and thinking that your boat has sunk. My mom is in her eighties and she is beautiful. I can see that at this age, you're just happy for the years the good Lord has given you and proud of the family legacy!

In each decade, the outer shell started changing and I had to love that girl in the mirror at forty, at fifty and now sixty. Yikes! The fine lines, spider veins (such an ugly name), the skin elasticity is going fast. I forget at times what I needed two minutes earlier, I really should not eat everything I want, and my sleepy time comes earlier at night! The gray hair is coming too fast, so gray I am, and gray I will stay. Hey, again, God is good! Gray hair is the new fad! People stop me and ask where I get my hair done. Really! I am not going to pay for gray hair, well not at this stage of my life. I still have to be sexy, but within the boundaries when it comes to clothes; but I still want to be sexy! I love being chic and sassy and knowing with confidence who I am!

Wow... changes, changes, changes, does it ever stop?! No, I have found out that it doesn't. Family challenges continue on a different level, but still valleys occur. I just have grown into a new comfort zone with God. Financially the ups are much longer than the downs, but they still can be rough when you are pulled so many ways if needed. The family needs you and you are the glue that holds things together. So, you better prepare yourself! Pray! Sex becomes this enchanting thing called making love. It is delightful to reach this period of intimacy. The love and awareness for one another is wonderful. No more worries... just enjoy this love that has matured and is rooted and is an amazing gift from God! No more worry about keeping up with the Barbie. I am the best real Barbie available. I hold up to heat, I can move, dance and sing. I can laugh, I can cook, I can multitask and make your head spin. And yes, I can still put on the pretty dress and high heels and make heads turn. I command attention because now my confidence is glowing, my joy is contagious, my favor is overflowing, I am living a life of excellence.

A good woman is hard to find and worth far more than diamonds! (Proverbs: 31:10, MSG) Diamonds are formed, not made. It takes years to be formed. Heat and pressure form diamonds. Diamonds are brought to the surface by major eruptions and disturbances. These are specific to each diamond. A diamond shines and is beautiful. Each diamond is rare. It is graded by color, clarity, cut and carats. The finest diamond is colorless, free of inclusions or blemishes. God has made us all fine diamonds. We are processed and cut perfectly, we have to go through the cleansing and purifying that gives us clarity of who and whose we are. We have carats of wisdom, knowledge, discernment, favor, mercy, and grace. When it comes to color, we are all unique. We have different skin color, different eye color and different hair color. God made us all! I love that God made sure each of us is a rare diamond.

Be proud of yourself. Never let society define you or make you feel unacceptable. God made you exactly how you should look. Beautiful, amazing, rare! We walk and we shine whenever we are present. We are the image of God! How awesome is that! We are the rarest jewel and God is so proud of who we are and who we have become. He loves us through our process because without it, we conform to our blemishes, but no need because Jesus came to remove each and every one. We don't have to compete or compare, we are unique, one of a kind! God presses us and forms us with all the eruptions and disturbances of life. He refines us in the heat and forms us by His love.

In the same way, the women are to be worthy of respect, not malicious talkers but temperate and trustworthy in everything.

1 TIMOTHY 3:11 (NIV)

Likewise, teach the older women to be reverent in the way they live, not to be slanderers or addicted to much wine, but to teach what is good. Then they can urge the younger women to love their husbands and children, to be self-controlled and pure, to be busy at home, to be kind, and to be subject to their husbands, so that no one will malign the word of God.

TITUS 2:3-5 (NIV)

A wife of noble character who can find? She is worth far more than rubies. Her husband has full confidence in her and lacks nothing of value. She brings him good, not harm, all the days of her life. She selects wool and flax and works with eager hands. She is like the merchant ships, bringing her food from afar. She gets up while it is still night, she provides food for her family and portions for

*her female servants. She considers a field and buys it; out
of her earnings she plants a vineyard. She sets about her
work vigorously; her arms are strong for her tasks. She sees
that her trading is profitable, and her lamp does not go out
at night. In her hand she holds the distaff and grasps the
spindle with her fingers. She opens her arms to the poor
and extends her hands to the needy. When it snows she
has no fear for her household; for all of them are clothed in
scarlet. She makes coverings for her bed; she is clothed in
fine linen and purple. Her husband is respected at the city
gate, where he takes his seat among the elders of the land.
She makes linen garments and sells them. And supplies
the merchants with sashes. She is clothed with strength
and dignity; she can laugh at the days to come. She speaks
with wisdom, and faithful instruction is on her tongue.
She watches over the affairs of her household and does
not eat the bread of idleness. Her children arise and call
her blessed; her husband also, and he praises her: "Many
women do noble things, but you surpass them all." Charm
is deceptive, and beauty is fleeting; but a woman who fears
the Lord is to be praised. Honor her for all her hands have
done, and let her works bring her praise at the city gate.*

PROVERBS 31:10-31 (NIV)

Did you read this? It's amazing. I love how it details us
completely. I love how we can work and be successful busi-
nesswomen, and still be wives. I love that we are creative
and talented. I love that we are called blessed. We are val-

ued and respected along with our husbands. We work hard and our hands are strong. We are noble and honored. Wow! Who couldn't love this woman?

CHAPTER FIFTEEN

Ok, But Naked?

So, we should love ourselves no matter what. Yes, my nakedness has changed, oh boy, what a change! Yes, I am going to get real before I wind down this book. I was a little thin thing, and it was nice. I ate everything I saw and
gained nothing when I was young. So, of course I thought
this would last forever. Forever changed. We are so anxious to be eighteen, twenty-one, thirty, that we don't enjoy
where we are. Our lives move so fast! We need to appreciate
today. Be thankful for today because we are only like this
today, we change and grow older tomorrow.

Now as you can see by my picture, I am gray. I was born
a brunette, then I graduated to a beautiful auburn-haired
woman. Then gradually I became blonde and gracefully
gray. So, you see, don't look at blondes and think they have
more fun, you might be one, one day! I laugh because I remember my mom's process and thought that would never
be me. I remember her changing her style of dress, longer sleeves, longer dress, and I laughed and thought, "Not
me." I love that she has always been so sophisticated, and

she paved the way for me to aging. She showed me how to be pretty with all my changes and to grow old with class. This body might change, but God made us just as we are. Varicose veins, marionette lines, nasolabial folds, elevens between brows, love handles, cellulite, crepey skin, turkey neck... well the list continues. How about this list: injectable filler, OnabotulinumtoxinA (botox), laser treatments, facelifts, chemical peels, and so much more. I can guarantee that you will have to deal with the first list of things, but who can afford the second list? Some of us will try, but it does not make you younger. I believe in eating well, being active, taking care of your skin and doing whatever to make yourself happy and help improve your confidence. Dress pretty, wear cute shoes, add the fun bling, smell good and always walk with confidence as if there is no one cuter than you in the room. Learn what looks good on you, not your friend's wardrobe. Get that great haircut and perfect length that fits you. Not every woman looks good with long hair! Wear your makeup well and learn your shades, especially lipstick. Learn the right lengths on that dress and how low the scoop should be on your blouse. Showing more isn't sexier! Feeling sexy is sexier, and you feel sexy when you know who you are, what you are, how to dress to complement your body. Smell good, have soft skin, a confident personality, and shine like a diamond. Have a feeling of accomplishment and put God in your heart and soul! Be the hands and feet of Christ and you will look amazing.

We were born naked. God wanted us to love ourselves that way. He did not want us to be ashamed. To hide our-

selves. Sin, shame, fear, anxiety, worry, confusion, inse-
curity, jealousy, competition, comparison, perverseness,
rejection has caused us to cover ourselves and feel ugly,
not worthy, not good, not acceptable, embarrassed, lonely. No more. Jesus removed it all on that cross. He said, "It
is finished!" No more shame, worry, or lacking anything.
He stripped all that away and left us free! Now of course,
we can't walk around naked, but we must walk around naked of all the negative thoughts that we hear and things we
believe about ourselves. We must strip ourselves naked of
shame, hatred, jealousy, sorrow, pain, anxiety, confusion.
Imagine the weight that this removes. Imagine how you
would look, how you would act, how great you would feel.
God can and will do it for you. He did it for me so He will
do it for you. Stay in prayer, ask Him for guidance. Expect
Him to show up and do great things for you and through
you. He removed all the bad when Jesus died on the cross,
sins were forgiven. He came to give us a life. Yes, a life filled
with abundance, joy, and all the good things when Jesus
rose out of that grave! Yes, we are so blessed! He calls us
His child! Now you know how much a parent wants to give
his child, so imagine how much our heavenly Father wants
to give us!

*And we all, who with unveiled faces contemplate the
Lord's glory, are being transformed into his image with
ever increasing glory, which comes from the Lord, who is
the Spirit.*

2 CORINTHIANS 3:18 (NIV)

*I praise you because I am fearfully and wonderfully made;
your works are wonderful, I know that full well.*

PSALMS 139:14 (NIV)

*"Indeed, the very hairs on your head are all numbered. Do
not be afraid; you are worth more than many sparrows."*

LUKE 12:7 (NIV)

*Then I observed that most people are motivated to success
because they envy their neighbors. But this, too, is mean-
ingless-like chasing the wind.*

ECCLESIASTES 4:4 (NLT)

Be Strong

Do not let satan compare you to this world we are living in. Do not let him steal one more minute of your life or joy. There will be no more destroying you because you are God's child, His favorite. The devil comes to steal, kill, and destroy. God came to give us a life of abundance. Stop listening to the devil whisper negative words and thoughts in your ear. Don't give him an opportunity to take your joy. For the joy of the Lord is your strength. Do not play those negative recordings over and over again in your mind. The devil is a liar! Cast him out of your life and listen no more to his lies about you. God has you forever in the palm of His hands. Remain there safe and secure. God is calling you wonderful, masterpiece, His child.

Imagine that we are children of the Most High God! We have His DNA and are heirs to everything! The devil hates that. That is why he tries so hard to confuse us, but no way, Devil. We serve a mighty God! Do not waiver right or left; stick to your lane and be happy in it. It is your life, your body, your happiness, don't imitate someone else! God made you just as He intended you to be. You are unique and have talents and attributes that He placed in you for specific reasons. Do not lower your standards, stay steadfast in what you believe. Do not give yourself to someone because you need to feel loved. Protect your body because you only have one. It is not an instrument to be used and then pushed to the side by someone who never cared. It is not a bargaining tool in a relationship. He will wait if he loves you! Ladies, I know it is hard to be celibate; we are human, but this is a decision that hurts deeply if the relationship does not work. You feel robbed of something precious. He does not deserve that part of you if he is not serious about you. You are only hurting yourself. But we hear this recording in our mind as Satan whispers them: I need to be accepted, I need love, I am lonely, I am hurt so I need someone to give me attention, I won't ever get married, I need that promotion, he said he loved me and I'm beautiful, he will find someone else if it's not me, I want to, I have physical needs. It's okay, the Bible is old and it's a new generation. While God is saying: *You are my prized possession, wait because I have a wonderful husband for you, you don't have to sleep your way to that promotion because I will promote you, come to me those who are lonely, tired, I will comfort you, you're my masterpiece, beautiful, smart, my heir. I accept you just as you are, and I am madly in love with you.* I understand and know that we are human, and we fail, but we have to strive on becoming the women God intended us to be. Thankfully, he understands and forgives. Do not walk away with guilt, shame, feeling exposed and rejected. Be strong; use your godly discernment and be everything God has called you to be! We must protect what God has made. Society tells us go ahead, sex is great and exciting with anyone, anytime or any place. Society glamorizes promiscuity but does not paint the ugly picture of pain, guilt, hurt, shame, regret, and unplanned pregnancies. What now? The wrong decision can lead to unwanted pregnancies, unwanted abortions, unwanted diseases, unwanted destruction.

Yes, our God in all his glory will forgive us and forget. But what is the cost to us to go down this path? These are serious situations that affect us enormously. I pray that these words will help someone who is reading this and needs to hear that God loves you! We can rest assured that our Heavenly Father still loves us. He is still on the throne, and He still forgives and forgets our sins. This is His promise. Yes and amen to all of His promises. Not some of them, but all of them. So, trust Him and forgive yourself. Be strong and stay pure until you are sure, and remember you are God's temple so protect it!

But among you there must not be even a hint of sexual immorality, or of any kind of impurity, or of greed, because these are improper for God's holy people.

EPHESIANS 5:3 (NIV)

Flee from sexual immorality. All other sins a person commits are outside the body, but whoever sins sexually, sins against their own body.

1 CORINTHIANS 6:18 (NIV)

Do you know that your bodies are temples of the Holy Spirit, who is in you, whom you have received from God? You are not your own; you were bought at a price. Therefore honor God with your bodies.

1 CORINTHIANS 6:19-20 (NIV)

CHAPTER SEVENTEEN

My New Beginning

My days are amazing, because I give God control of each one of them. **Psalm 118:24 This is the day that the Lord has made; let us rejoice and be glad in it (ESV)!**

I wake up and thank the Lord every day for my husband, children, grandchildren, home, food, church, friends, country, my freedom, my salvation. Now please understand I still have problems and struggles, but I do not dwell on them anymore. I chose to be happy and content and thankful. Reprogram your thinking! Do not dwell on your circumstances. You have a choice each morning how you want to face the day. Face it with joy and expectation of God's blessings. You are equipped to fulfill your journey. My joy is permanent because my God is! My grandsons are precious. Luke is five and Nate is four years old, and baby Noah is 3 months old. I relive my kids in each of their faces and gestures. They are God's gift to me, and I receive it with a full heart. I still take care of one grandson full time and handle my two businesses. I still do real estate when I want to but not because I have to. Thank God! I hated menopause and all my skin changes. I took what the devil meant for harm and created my own line of natural body products. They are great and have improved my skin, and I am thankful for that.

You see, God is so good, he gives us double for our trouble. My business is doing good, but I expect God to make it great in his time. I enjoy my garden, cooking, cleaning, washing, and all that jazz but now I am grateful for strong hands, feet, eyes, and heart to do it all. I enjoy my days with my dearest friends. We take our grandchildren to museums, the library, pool, playground. I am loving this phase of my life. I have also learned that you have to select your friends wisely because you will do life with them. There is no time for jealousy or envy, just love and support! I am thankful because I get to do all these things, I get to love and care, protect, and pray over my loved ones. I have an abundance of joy, favor, mercy, and grace. I am all God intended me to be. I speak words of faith over myself and family.

We were married during the holidays on December 30, 1994 and that adds so much fun for me. We renewed our vows on our 20th anniversary in Hawaii. We had so much fun that we decided to renew our vows again for our 25th anniverary, this time with friends and family. I was abe to walk down the aisle with my kids and grandsons to meet that wonderful man at the altar one more time. That aisle has been pave with lots of great moments and adventures. I love that I get to run off with him and enjoy a romantic, intimate honeymoon again and again! Memories, legacies, and love...better than Hallmark!

Oh, about the ex, we try to get along! We have even done business together. I always included him in every party or holiday and my kids' functions. We married young and it just was not the right time. It is comforting that God healed all the past. He really loves his kids. It can be difficult because we are totally different in parenting, but I try for the kids. Do not be angry, do not be rude after a divorce as it only hurts the kids. I found that by accepting him being around my kids when they were young, they are more confident and secure. Plus, they love me for doing it. They never had to choose, and they have a great dad and father. We both have moved on and we love and care about our children and grandchildren just in different ways!

There will be more stories, valleys and successes and I have high expectations from my God. *My cup is running over and surely, goodness, and mercy will follow me all the days of my life* (Psalm 23:6). This body of mine is a story. The story goes like this... I have aged gracefully, full of love and passion. I have bounced back and been strong. I have loved, given of myself and shared. I have an amazing husband, children, and grandsons. I will serve my God and give Him all glory all the days of my life. I will go from Glory to Glory. My hair is gray because it is the sign of much wisdom. My frown lines are smile lines from joy. My body is an indication that I have had a long full life and shows I am a mom of excellence! So now when I look in the mirror, I see that painting of my life. I see every decade, every challenge, every change, every season. I see love, I see hope, I see resilience, I see me! I love me! God loves me! I love myself naked!

I hope this story of my life will help you! I tried to be real and open so that you might receive the blessing that you need. All has gone well, or at least I accept struggles easier because I know how great my God is and He will work it all out. Always remember how big your God is! I get up so much faster after a fall and choose to stay at ease during all my circumstances. I have so much more peace in my challenges now. I understand that there will be changes and that it is okay. I trust God for everything. I listen to that "still small voice," the Holy Spirit, and I lean in to hear every word He tells me. I love the scripture Psalm 23:2 *He maketh me to lie down in green pastures: he leadeth me beside the still waters* (KJV). Amen! Let Him give you rest, peace and ease. Let the Holy Spirit dwell in you, invite Him in and let it reveal glorious things to you. The Holy Spirit is a gift from God and is a guide for us to listen to and obey! The Holy Spirit will comfort you. He will be our intercessor. When we have no idea how to pray, the Holy Spirit does. The Holy Spirit is God in action. His power overtaking us and dwelling in us. He will guide us to the right path. He will strengthen us for battle. He will teach us what is right for us, what is pure and fair. The Holy Spirit lives in us! That "still small voice" is a powerful force in us. Listen, receive, and obey!

CHAPTER SIXTEEN

I praise you because I am fearfully and wonderfully made;
your works are wonderful, I know that full well.

PSALMS 139:14 (NIV)

O Lord, you have searched me and known me. You know
my sitting down and my rising up; You understand my
thought afar off. You comprehend my path and my lying
down, and are acquainted with all my ways. For there is
not a word on my tongue, but behold, O Lord, you know it
altogether.

PSALMS 139:1-4 (NKJV)

For I know the thoughts that I think toward you, says the
Lord, thoughts of peace and not of evil, to give you a future
and a hope. Then you will call upon Me and go and pray to
Me, and I will listen to you.

JEREMIAH 29:11-13 (NKJV)

Testimonies & Declarations

The following are from very dear family and friends of mine. These are testimonials of their experiences of having to learn to love themselves naked, raw, and exposed. I hope you gain encouragement from their words.

M. Blevins–

Learning to love and appreciate myself. However, it has taken some time to get to this point. It was through some mistakes, and by mistakes, I mean through men, the constant attention I received when men found out I was single. Sure, this boosted my confidence a bit. I no longer felt like the ugly new mom who couldn't possibly be attractive. After all, I am no model. But the praise and attention helped.

Learning to love myself naked in all forms is still a process for me. We see through the eyes of love. This is a phrase that I have been told so many times by a ton of people. But what exactly does it mean? When I first met my ex-husband, my cousins would joke around and say, "Man, you must really love him if you think he's attractive." I would find that as time went on, and my love grew for him, the more attractive he became to me. Now, I'm not exactly sure how that works, but it does. So naturally, I assumed that it worked the same way for him. As the days went on and his love grew for me, he too would see me the same way I saw him, with this immense amount of love and adoration. He made me feel this way for a long time, even during "most" of my pregnancy. When I was six months pregnant, my ex and I went through a rough patch that lasted about two weeks. He seemed a little distant, more like distracted. When I asked him what was going on, he would tell me that he was a little confused and not sure what he wanted for his life. Now, again, I was six months pregnant! I had no idea where this was coming from. We were happy. How could he feel this way? After about two weeks of this awkward phase in our lives, he bounced back rather quickly and was 100 percent on board and excited about this little bundle of joy that was on the way. I just assumed, along with the rest of my family, that he probably got nervous and then snapped out of it. Well, immediately after our son was born, my ex-husband walked out on us. Talk about completely un-expected. Shortly after our separation, he met a girl. She was about six years younger than he was, so that was about nine years younger than me. She was an Instagram model. Oh, and a stripper. What a male fantasy right? Well, here's the deal, I'm not an Instagram model or a stripper. Thank God for that! I was a new mom, with a new body that I was learning to like, and attention just didn't seem to fill this void that was inside of me. There was still this feeling of emptiness; am I good enough, am I pretty enough, am I smart enough? My mom gave me several scripture cards during my separation. She has no idea how much I depended on them. Here are three of those scriptures that I would keep on me everywhere I went:

"...My grace is all you need.
My power works best in weakness."

2 CORINTHIANS 12:9 (NLT)

"Don't be afraid, for I am with you.
Don't be discouraged, for I am your God."

ISAIAH 41:10 (NLT)

"God is our merciful Father and the source
of all comfort."

2 CORINTHIANS 1:3 (NLT)

I have learned that there is not a man in this world that can fill any void of mine. It comes from God, and God alone. He is my strength. He is my comfort. I will not be discouraged, for He is my God. And what an amazing God He is! He blessed me with my beautiful baby boy Luke, who I give 100 percent credit to for my new mom bod. He is totally worth it. I am still a work in progress, but every day I am learning to love this new and improved godly woman that was pieced together so perfectly by my heavenly Father.

W. Ortiz–

I felt fearless naked and raw. It has been such a long road full of potholes and rough patches, but I'm overjoyed that God has delivered me to this place where fear doesn't control me. Growing up, I had a spirit of fear that controlled me so much I didn't even play a sport. I couldn't take part in the fun ones that didn't even count the score or announced a winner or loser because I thought surely there will still be something wrong with me. I would be to blame for losing it for the team.

In high school, I remembered that I didn't genuinely make lifelong friends because I feared they would tell my secrets or talk about me behind my back. Moving onto college I had my heart set on being a registered nurse, but I switched to a different major because I feared getting rejected from nursing school. Fear was running my life and I didn't even know that it was.

I worked full time and attended college while serving in the National Guard. It would seem that maybe I had conquered this fear, but I hadn't. I would be so afraid that my schedule at work would clash with school and the National Guard that I had a breakdown every semester. But as always, God worked it out and I was able to graduate with honors.

When I was working as a National Guard recruiter, I came upon a Bible verse that was so very life-changing for me. I was a new Christ follower and being in a job that required a quota was so challenging. Psalm 118:6 The Lord is on my side; I will not fear. What can man do to me? (NKJV)

At that moment I knew I could try my hardest and fail and the Lord would still be by my side. Words cannot express how thankful I am about not being that fearful woman any longer. I am blessed to be a wife to an amazing husband and a mom to an incredible little boy. I believe the Lord allowed me to be able to receive these blessings when I could handle them. I know that not in my own power but in His that I will be able to conquer what He gives me, with Him and not alone.

P. Brown –

Initially when I agreed to do this testimonial for my great friend, Monique Burks, I thought about what it meant to be in a book. How many people will see my truth? Am I really ready to be naked, raw and exposed? The answer is YES! For years I would hide when someone found out the truth about me. Especially if it was something that I wanted to hide. I was molested at seven by a female friend of my family. Later my virginity was stolen by a family member. Once I entered high school, I became friends with someone who later got drunk and raped me. Then the ultimate act of betrayal was when I was date raped by a boyfriend. This encounter left me with a baby who I was too afraid to abort.

I suffered greatly throughout my life. It left me so afraid to be exposed by anyone. I lived defending myself. Hating men wanted to vindicate the abuse that I suffered at the hands of those I trusted. It was not until the year 2010 as I faced a turning point in my life. I got word that my marriage had been legally dissolved. I felt as though I had no clothes on in a sea of people. That everyone saw my flaws, scares and the truth of what my clothes had been able to hide. For months I did not set foot in the local church, take anyone's phone calls or connect with people who knew that had happened. It was not until July 9, 2011 that I could no longer hide. That day at 6:53 a.m. my former husband passed away. Facing the music now was no longer an option but mandatory! I had to deal with his family that never cared for me. Recall everything that I hated about him all while giving my all to see to it that he was laid to rest properly. I was crushed under the weight of the pain of the past. Vulnerable, saddened, hurt, betrayed... I mean the list of emotions were just horrible. Not to mention the suffering that my dear children would have to face. Although I had a challenging union, he was a fantastic father! To answer the question now in 2019, how do I feel naked, raw and exposed? Relieved is the first word that comes to mind. No longer hiding from people's opinion of me. Unashamed of where I have been or the errors that I made in times past. Just to be nude is a graceful state to exist in nothing to worry about. I mean you cannot get any more transparent than that. It is liberating to just be me. Open, honest, loyal, loved, respected and admired. Fear is no longer my friend

I have accepted me for me. I intend to become the better version of myself each, and every day! I pray that this testimonial blesses you like it did me to write about my nudity which gives me yet another layer of freedom.

Scriptures to keep on hand when needed. I pray you will use them and they will comfort you through your valleys! This is how I fight my battles!

"No weapon that is formed against you will prosper"

ISAIAH 54:17 (NASB1995)

"Give all your worries and cares to God,
for he cares about you."

1 PETER 5:7 (NLT)

"And the God of all grace, who called you to his eternal
glory in Christ, after you have suffered a little while,
will himself restore you and make you strong,
firm and steadfast."

1 PETER 5:10 (NIV)

"Surely your goodness and unfailing love will pursue me
all the days of my life, and I will live in the house of the
Lord forever."

PSALMS 23:6 (NLT)

"Praise the Lord! For he has heard my cry for mercy. The Lord is my strength and shield. I trust him with all my heart. He helps me, and my heart is filled with joy. I burst out in songs of thanksgiving."

PSALMS 28:6-7 (NLT)

"He alone is my rock and my salvation, my fortress where I will not be shaken."

PSALMS 62:6 (NLT)

"Don't worry about anything; instead, pray about everything. Tell God what you need, and thank him for all he has done."

PHILIPPIANS 4:6 (NLT)

"For we are God's masterpiece. He has created us anew in Christ Jesus, so we can do the good things he planned for us long ago."

EPHESIANS 2:10 (NLT)

"I can do all things through Him who strengthens me."

PHILIPPIANS 4:13 (NASB1995)

"Trust in the Lord with all your heart; do not depend on your own understanding."

PROVERBS 3:5 (NLT)

"...If God is for us, who can be against us?"

ROMANS 8:31 (NIV)

"And my God will supply all your needs according to His riches in glory in Christ Jesus."

PHILIPPIANS 4:19 (NASB1995)

"Therefore I tell you, whatever you ask for in prayer, believe that you have received it, and it will be yours."

MARK 11:24 (NIV)

"For I am the Lord your God who takes hold of your right hand and says to you, Do not fear; I will help you."

ISAIAH 41:13 (NIV)

"I instruct you in the way of wisdom and lead you along straight paths."

PROVERBS 4:11 (NIV)

"God is our refuge and strength, an ever-present help in trouble."

PSALMS 46:1 (NIV)

Speak These Declarations Over Yourself:

I am God's masterpiece!

I am beautiful!

I am wonderfully made!

I am strong!

I am courageous!

I am redeemed!

I am motivated!

I am confident!

I am anointed!

I am blessed!

I have favor!

I have grace!

I have mercy!

I am victorious!

I am the head not the tail!

I am smart!

I am approved!

I am unique!

I am powerful!

I am a child of the Most High God!

I am the heir of God!

I am secure and full of joy!

Come to the Father!

The ultimate stripping naked occurred on that cross. Jesus was stripped, beaten, humiliated and exposed. He hung there in pain for our sins. He rose to give us life, to live abundantly. We are never alone. If you feel naked, raw, and exposed, rest assure that God covers you with His blood and the Holy Spirit will give you comfort and peace.

"And now, dear brothers and sisters, one final thing. Fix your thoughts on what is true, and honorable, and right, and pure, and lovely, and admirable. Think about things that are excellent and worthy of praise."

PHILIPPIANS 4:8 (NLT)

"But if we confess our sins to him, he is faithful and just to forgive us our sins and to cleanse us from all wickedness."

1 JOHN 1:9 (NLT)